Breaking the Broken

Debunking the Myth of Social Justice

Rob Kendall

Carpenter's Son Publishing

Published in Franklin, TN by Carpenter's Son Publishing

Edited by Christy Callahan
Cover Image by Royce DeGrie – DeGriephoto.com
Cover Design by Suzanne Lawing

ISBN 978-0-9881952-6-4

CSP

CONTENTS

ACKNOWLEDGEMENTS

Thank you to my incredible other half, Meredith. I can't imagine walking the road God has brought me down without you. You are an inspiration, the love of my life, and the only person that can really get under my skin. Thanks to my kids and grands for putting up with my babbling thoughts and understanding why your mother and I are consumed in ministry. You have given me a full heart, insight into life, and so much material. Thanks to Dr. Chris Williamson for your sermons that helped confirm what God was teaching Meredith and I about radically living for Him. I can't tell you the number of times Meredith would look at me during a sermon and say, "Has he been reading your journal?" Bart and Tammy, no one knows this journey better than you two. You have been there from the beginning and your friendships continues to be a gift from God. Thanks to Adam, Zach, Michael, Ramon, Stu, and Paul for being the iron in my life, my sounding boards, and a source of encouragement. Thanks to my board for your support in directing Against the Grain and Renewing The Mind Network. Last, but certainly the greatest, thanks to God the Father, Jesus Christ, His Son, and the Holy Spirit for drawing me, accepting me, and filling me for ministry.

PREFACE

Many Christians believe social justice displays God's love. They believe it benefits those who are served. They believe it is the example Jesus gave in His own life. But those are all misconceptions. Social justice does none of these things.

Social justice is demeaning. Social justice creates hierarchy. Social justice creates division. Social justice is transactional. Social justice is hopeless. Social justice does not work and is further breaking those who are broken.

We spend astronomical sums of money on social welfare programs, but what are the results? Is life getting better for those in poverty? Are the numbers decreasing? Are we making any significant progress? In the war on poverty, poverty has won. The benefits of social justice are a myth. The experiment has failed, but God has a plan.

God's plan offers dignity. God's plan creates equality. God's plan creates unity. God's plan is relational. God's plan offers hope. God's plan has worked in centuries past and will work again. God does not call us to social justice—He calls us to heal the broken.

Over these next pages, you'll learn about God's plan. You'll learn the what, who, why, where, how, and when. You'll see His plan in action. You'll see the hope God's plan provides. Your mission, if you choose to accept it, is to take God's plan to the lost and hurting and heal what is broken.

CHAPTER 1

THE AMERICAN DREAM

The men were tending the grill and getting out footballs, chalk, and games for the kids while the women were busy setting out paper plates, plastic utensils, and all the sides and condiments. We were ready to have a great time. We had been told there could be as many as twenty to thirty people who might come, but we didn't really know what to expect. I was nervous to say the least.

I thought there might be a problem. To be perfectly honest the white, middle-class, paranoid, suburban side of me wondered if we would get out of there alive. It was June 4, 2003, and my wife (Meredith) and I were hosting a cookout. It wasn't uncommon for us to enjoy a meal with friends (although we usually went to a decent restaurant for dinner), but this was quite different. Just a few weeks earlier our dinner guests would have been people who looked like us, thought like us, and wore the same name brands as us, but not this night. I can't speak for anyone else in our group, but for the first time in my life, I would be the minority.

Not only were our dinner guests outside our norm, but we were hosting this party in a park. Not in the well-furnished sports park or the neighborhood park with its perfectly manicured Bermuda grass that was just a short walk from our house. No,

5

those parks were on our turf and would have added a little comfort to the evening. This park was home to a few run-down toys and a small pavilion that had been tagged with spray paint and showed the signs of its age. This was the inner-city park located next to the housing projects.

It wasn't the first time Meredith and I had been in this part of Franklin. We had gone into "that" part of town a few times when our church had been involved in some events. We had been part of prayer walks and the annual Martin Luther King March in this area, but on those occasions we were part of a larger group. We attended a racially diverse church and hung out with a racially diverse crowd. I felt like we were invited into the neighborhood for those events to show our support.

I often drove through this area. The main road that went through the projects connected two of the major roads in Franklin. Sometimes I drove through because it was just a shortcut and other times because my curiosity got the best of me. I often wondered what life would be like living down there. During those quick drives through the projects, I tried not to look nervous and always locked my doors.

This night was different, though. We weren't part of a big group, we weren't quickly driving through the neighborhood, and we didn't have the safety of locked doors. There were only a few of us: Meredith, our three daughters, and me; my accountability partner, his wife, and their three kids; and a couple of other friends from church. It wasn't going to be a short walk through the community. We were staying for a while and we were in *their* park. How did we get here? Just a year and a half earlier I never could have imagined this would be the result. Our lives were perfect and we were living for Christ, or so I thought.

We had made it. We had achieved our dream life. We had three beautiful daughters, a phenomenal church, and good friends (many of whom also happened to be famous). We owned two businesses and a nice house in the county, but to think that our lives couldn't get any better was not the case. We were looking to expand my business, Meredith's real-estate career continued to grow, and she was becoming nationally recognized for her abilities. We loved our house, but we were preparing to build our dream home in an exclusive neighborhood. We had it all: the family, the careers, the church, the community, and the friends. The only thing left was to build and fill our new home and garage with all the latest gadgets and toys. We were living and loving the American Dream.

While all of this may sound a little selfish, we were extremely active serving others. We used the resources we had been given to support our church, and we had even committed to give more than 10 percent of our income to the work of God's kingdom. We led Bible studies and sang in the choir, and our kids were involved in ministry as well. We supported both local and overseas ministries and opened our home to pregnant mothers who needed a safe place to live. We were not the type of family that only "talked the talk"—we "walked the walk" too.

We had a good plan in place to continue enjoying our lives and serving the kingdom of God. That is until January 2002. It was a beautiful, but cold, sunny Monday morning. The kids were on the bus, Meredith was on her way to a meeting, and I had just finished loading my truck and was heading toward the job site. Meredith called with a request that would change the future of our lives.

She didn't start with any pleasantries. There was no *good morning* or *hi*, just a simple statement: "If this is the American Dream, we've been lied to." It took me a little off guard, but I was sure this must be some kind of response to a New Year's resolution. It was January after all, but she went on. "I want you to close your business, take a year off of work, and figure out what God wants to do with this family."

That was a ridiculous idea and my response was immediate: "No!" I loved our lives and was not interested in disrupting the status quo, but Meredith was convinced we needed a change. In order to keep the peace, I agreed to talk about it, but I had no intention of ever really discussing it, let alone giving it a second thought. I was sure this was just an emotional wave that would soon go away, but Meredith would not let it rest. So we talked.

Our talks turned into conversations, our conversations turned into discussions, and our discussions turned into arguments. We spent the next few weeks fighting about her demands. In mid-February I was done with the entire topic and put my foot down. In a desperate attempt to end the discussion, once and for all, I made my declaration: "I am the head of this household and the leader of this family and I am NOT closing my business." I could tell those words hurt her, but I was sure that this was over.

She looked at me and said, "You're right. You are the head of this household and the leader of this family." I couldn't hold back the slight grin that appeared on my face. I had won. This was finally going to end, but she continued, "Now lead us spiritually."

That hurt. I thought I had done a good job of being the spiritual leader of our family. We were active in all forms of ministry and so were our kids, but obviously she wanted more. At that moment I realized the conversation was over, but the tables had suddenly turned. I was not on the winning end. I was going to take a sabbatical.

I always began the New Year with a light work schedule, so closing my business was pretty easy. I took the next six weeks to finish up a couple of projects and didn't accept any new work. I wasn't happy about it and I really didn't know what was supposed to happen, but on April 1, 2002, I began a one-year sabbatical in search of God's will for our family. That year ended up being an incredible, painful season, but it changed our lives.

The sabbatical got off to a slow start. I had no idea how I was supposed to discover God's will and, to be perfectly honest, I fell asleep every time I tried to read or pray. My method of Bible study didn't help much either. I used what I now refer to as the "point and click" method. I would open the Bible and point at a passage, expecting God to show me His master plan for our lives in a single instance through divine intervention. You can imagine how well that went.

After a couple of weeks, I decided to add a little structure to my reading. I had always wanted to read the Bible all the way through and figured if God was going to show me something, the answer was probably going to come from the Bible. I did the math and figured out that if I read just a few chapters a day, I could read through the entire Bible in a year. I began that morning with a simple prayer: *Lord, show me Your heart.* That was the day the sabbatical really began.

In the first few chapters of Genesis, I saw some really interesting things I had never seen before. So I followed a few references, looked up some words in the original language, and continued reading and studying. I thought about stopping at the end of chapter 5, but didn't have anything else to do, and I was getting drawn into the Word, so I kept reading. I found themes as I read and continued to see them again and again. Every so often I would come to the end of a chapter, story, or section and think about stopping, but I didn't. I just kept reading. The longer I read, the more I wanted to read.

As I finished chapter 50 of Genesis, I heard the squeal of brakes from the bus as the kids arrived home from school. I couldn't believe it. I hadn't fallen asleep, I hadn't been distracted, and I hadn't even stopped for lunch. I had read the entire book of Genesis in a span of nearly six hours. I hadn't skipped over the genealogies and those themes kept showing up. I put my stuff to the side and spent the afternoon with the girls.

That evening after dinner, I excused myself from our normal routine of homework and TV and went back to review some of what I had read earlier that day. This was before I had a good Bible on my laptop, or resources on the Internet, so I got out all of my study materials and spread them out on the dining room table. I was fully engrossed in checking, referencing, and cross-referencing from dictionaries, concordances, commentaries, and different versions of the Bible. I began asking questions about what I was reading. Why was this written? How would this passage be different if I were part of the original audience? Were there specific circumstances being addressed, or was this an eternal lesson?

Meredith checked on me a couple of times to see if I was OK or if I wanted to join them. The girls gave me hugs and kisses and said their good-nights. Meredith came up at eleven o'clock and asked if I was coming to bed. I told her I wanted to finish studying a couple of things and would be to bed soon. When I looked up a few minutes later, it was two o'clock in the morning, so I put away my study materials and headed to bed.

I have never been a morning person and often don't like life before 10:00 a.m., but when the alarm went off at 6:00 a.m., I was wide awake. I had gone to bed only four hours earlier, but had no desire to go back to sleep. I wanted to get back to Scripture and pick up where I had left off the night before. I read the entire book of Exodus while the girls were at school and spent the night referencing and cross-referencing.

This became my pattern for the remainder of the year. Reading and studying consumed most of my time. My prayer life came alive and I would spend hours talking with God. There were days when I read entire books of the Bible and weeks when I wrestled with a small section of Scripture. I asked questions of the Bible and looked for flaws in the easy answers I had grown accustom to accepting.

The next twelve months shattered the perfect life I thought we had. In many ways, I met God for the very first time. The familiar stories in the Bible became living words. I saw God in all His glory and power. I saw His righteousness, holiness, and love. I learned I had trusted God with eternity, but did not trust Him with my day-to-day life.

I saw the blind obedience and sacrifice of His children in Scripture. When God said "Go," they went. In most cases there is no evidence that they questioned or argued. They just obeyed. I saw God's faithful love and care for His people, and it became easier to understand their blind obedience. God always came through. When God was their only hope, God was all they needed.

As I reflected on my walk with God compared to those I was reading about in Scripture, I came to some painful realizations. My faith was immature at best. It was nothing more than a lifestyle that suited me well. I was selfish and my heart beat only for me. I knew the promises that benefited me, but didn't want to respond with a life of sacrifice. I realized I was merely a "comfortable" Christian if such a thing really exists. I learned that I was more in love with grace than I was with Christ.

God showed me that He had a plan for our lives. He had created us for a purpose. My spiritual life would no longer be something I had to do, but a passion that burned deep within me. My life would change to reflect God's plan for our family. While there is nothing wrong with making a lot of money and having nice things, the pursuit of these things would no longer be our highest priority. Our Christianity had filled our calendars with activities based around the church, but we were not making a difference in our community and we were not making a difference for Christ. We came up with the motto "Against the Grain" based on Romans 12.

Therefore, brothers, by the mercies of God, I urge you to present your bodies as a living sacrifice, holy and pleasing to God; this is your spiritual worship. Do not be conformed to this age, but be transformed by the renewing of your mind, so that you may discern what is the good, pleasing, and perfect will of God. (Rom. 12:1–2)

We were going to worship God with our daily lives. We did not need the latest and greatest gadgets, and we were not going to buy our dream home in the exclusive community. We were going to live differently and our priorities would change. We were no longer going to go with the flow of society or the "comfortable" Christian lifestyle we had come to know and love. We were going to live "Against the Grain."

Even though we had a new outlook on life, I still had no idea where God was leading us. It was March and I only had a couple of weeks left to figure it out. I could easily reopen my business, but that just didn't feel right. God was changing our course. I began to wonder if God was preparing me to write and preach, which made sense. My great grandfather had been a circuit preacher and my grandfather had been an evangelist. Maybe God was calling me to challenge believers to radically submit their lives to Christ, and to encourage them to walk away from the same lukewarm faith I had lived just a year earlier.

With only ten days left in the sabbatical, I began to get anxious, and wondered when God was going to give me a crystal-clear direction on where He was leading our family. We were ready to blindly obey like the heroes of our faith, but we needed to know where we were going. Meredith and Amanda (our oldest) were going on a women's retreat, and I figured this would be a good weekend to pray for direction. I have heard it said that God is never early and God is never late, but He is always on time. That weekend He gave us marching orders for our next adventure in life, although they weren't packaged the way I expected them to be.

A young woman from a Bible study that Meredith was leading at church wanted to go to the women's retreat, but needed a ride. We owned two vehicles, a van and a truck, and because I was going to be home with two of the girls, Meredith would be taking the truck. She was more than happy to find a ride for our oldest daughter, who was beginning her rebellious stage, and help this young mother with transportation. When Meredith drove into the neighborhood, she realized that this young lady lived in public housing.

The theme of the women's retreat was "Passing the Baton to the Next Generation." They studied a passage in Titus 2 that calls older women to mentor younger women. The older women are supposed to walk with the younger woman and train them to be godly wives and mothers. They also heard a story about a butterfly and how breaking open a cocoon to help the young butterfly get out can actually weaken and endanger it. Meredith learned that the butterfly gains its strength to fly through the fight to break free from the cocoon.

During one of the session breaks, Amanda was in Meredith's face, saying, "You can't tell me what to do. Just leave me alone. I can make my own decisions." You know, the normal stuff for a rebellious teenager. Well, this young mother looked at Amanda and said, "If I only had a mother like yours, I wouldn't be where I am today." In the excitement of the weekend, Meredith replied, "I'll be your mom."

Meredith called me and said, "I think we've adopted someone." Now, the idea of adoption was not new. We had talked about adoption, but my heart had always been towards adopting a child from Haiti. She went on, "But there's a catch. She comes with three boys." I panicked. I've heard about the crazy things that happen on women's retreats. Trying to remain calm, I told her we could talk about it when she got home.

When Meredith came home on Sunday afternoon, she told me this young lady's story. She was a third-generation single mother, who was living in public housing and had dropped out of high school in the tenth grade because she had gotten pregnant. Currently at the age of 23, she had three children from two different men and there was no father figure in the home. She had no career, no education, and no hope. She was tired and wanted a chance at a different life.

When I heard her story, I knew exactly what to do. During the last year God had shown me a lot about Himself, but He had also given me insights into His plan for serving the poor. It was as if a thousand puzzle pieces had been floating above my head and suddenly dropped into place, allowing me to clearly see the picture. I ran downstairs, flipped open my laptop, and wrote out a plan. Ten minutes later I handed it to Meredith and she started crying. "This is exactly what I thought we should do," she said. We called the young mother and invited her and her children to come to our home for dinner.

After dinner we talked about how we could help her overcome the challenges that were holding her down. We told her we would not give her money, but would walk with her and help her gain what she needed to live independently. We would watch her children if she was going to school or work and open up our circle of influence to help her find a job. We would help her gain what she needed to stand on her own, and we would do it all from a biblical perspective, but she would have to do the hard work. We would help her, but she would be responsible for her decisions and making the necessary changes in her life.

This young mother accepted the help and quickly found a job. Meredith and I provided transportation and childcare. She began to see hope, but we were running ourselves ragged trying to keep her schedule as well as our own. We needed to figure out a way to work this differently. Since we had been talking about hiring an assistant for Meredith, we offered the job to our new friend. She accepted and our calendars began to make more sense.

One morning in May she came to work and said, "I have some friends who want what I have." Meredith told her, "I can't hire anybody else." She said, "No...they want you." Meredith and I talked and agreed to meet with her friends. We needed a place where the moms could bring their kids, so we decided to have a cookout in the park.

That's where I found myself that night: cooking hamburgers and hotdogs in a park that was completely foreign to me. Looking back, I'm not sure if I was more nervous about being in "that" part of town or opening up our lives to complete strangers. Either way, I was filled with apprehension. The food was almost ready as the women began showing up with their kids. Introductions were being made. There was no turning back now.

We all had an incredible time getting to know our new friends. We talked with the moms and played games with the kids. There were no issues with the community, and within a few minutes I didn't even think about being outside of our comfort zone. It just felt right. After dinner, while the kids were swinging, spinning on the merry-go-round, and playing football, we shared our vision. They were more receptive than I had imagined.

I figured a few of them might be interested, and I figured a few of them would want nothing to do with it. Boy was I wrong. They *all* wanted in. Every last one of them said, "*Yes*, we want the help." Our little commitment to walk with one single mom and her three kids had just exploded. We were now committing our lives to nine moms with twenty-eight kids.

Meredith and I went home that night stunned. We were both excited and completely terrified by the positive response. We realized this was so much bigger than we were and we needed to get some structure around it. While both of us had run our own businesses, neither of us had experience setting up something like this. So we asked for advice from our friends and the churches we were associated with.

Our friends gave us mixed responses. Some supported the idea, even though they didn't understand the passion, but others were against it. "Rob, God has given you abilities in remodeling and craftsmanship. Go back to work and take care of your family. It shouldn't be on Meredith to provide. You're the husband and you should be leading your family." Meredith was told similar things. "God has gifted you with the ability to make a lot of money, so don't get distracted. Make as much as you can to support the kingdom."

I met with my pastor and another local church that actively served in the community. As I prepared for each of these meetings, I was sure that they would be excited about the opportunity to serve single mothers and their kids. I told them the whole story of the last year and a half and how we believed this was God's calling on our lives. I laid out our vision to help these women get on their feet and provide independently for their families and asked how we could run this through the church. I couldn't believe the responses.

While these are not direct quotes, here are some of the things that were said by both churches. "It won't work. We have been trying to help these women for years and they won't change. They'll just take advantage of you. They don't want the help. Rob, you've heard about the plight of the African American community and you want to do something, but this is just white guilt. Go back to work and take care of your family."

Meredith and I are pretty straightforward people. We don't believe in hiding things to keep up appearances, so we went to the moms and told them what the churches said. We asked them to be upfront with us. If they were not going to be serious, if they really didn't want to change, we wanted to know ahead of time. No harm, no foul. Just let us know if we are wasting our time.

Their response hurt, but confirmed everything I had read over the last year. "We don't trust the churches anyways," they said. "They come in, start a program, and we get all excited because we begin to believe our lives could actually change. Then something happens. The pastor moves, the budget is cut, a volunteer leaves, and we are left hanging. So we get out of the church what we can get out of the church."

Meredith and I learned two important lessons from this experience that have shaped our lives moving forward. First, we will follow God's call regardless of the consequences. We talked through the implications of serving these women on a full-time basis. We may lose friends, money, and status; we may be misunderstood, ridiculed, or even harmed, but if we had to make a choice between pleasing God and pleasing people, we would choose God every time. Second, our service to the poor had been counterproductive. We were making things worse and adding to their struggle. We were actually breaking the broken. Trying to make someone more comfortable in a life that is falling apart isn't really helping.

I once heard a man speak on serving the poor. He said Jesus would have climbed down into the mud and the mire to be with people. While this is true, I had learned Jesus didn't want them to stay in the mud and the mire. He would have helped them get out. Meredith and I were going to start a ministry to do just that. We were going to work with these women, and others in the community, to help them end their struggles.

Our motto to live "Against the Grain" became the name of the ministry. I spent the next few months learning all I could about becoming a nonprofit. I completed the paperwork, submitted it, and six-weeks and four days later we were approved as a 501(c)(3) not-for-profit organization. Meredith and I led Bible studies with the moms while our girls tutored the kids. The moms began to see changes in their lives, and the request for training continued to grow.

God has blessed this effort in ways I could never have imagined. What began as simple Bible lessons to help single moms understand and achieve their unique God-given potential has become a series of studies that are spreading across the country. These studies are being used in churches, jails, prisons, halfway houses, homeless shelters, and crisis pregnancy and recovery centers to provide hope to thousands of people every year. Lives are being changed, families are being restored, and hope is being offered to those who are willing to do the hard work. The reading and homework assistance our girls offered to their kids has grown into its own organization providing one-on-one tutoring to hundreds of children in two school districts.

For more than a decade, Against the Grain has used God's plan as our structure in ministry. We use the plan He showed me to care for the poor with amazing results. Hope is being brought to the hopeless, addictions are being broken, and lives are being changed. It's not easy, it doesn't always feel good, but it works. It is hard and it hurts when you see a friend return to an addiction or an abusive relationship, but God never said serving Him would be easy.

If you're looking for a book full of ministry ideas that are easy to swallow, this is probably not the book for you, and I ask you to prayerfully keep an open mind as you move forward. What you read may sound harsh or even cold hearted at times, but love isn't always nice. You may get your toes stepped on a time or two, and you might even get offended. That's OK. Chewing and swallowing the meat of Scripture is harder than gulping down the milk. As you move forward, I ask you to begin with the simple prayer that I said early in the sabbatical: *Lord, show me Your heart.* It might be painful, it might be hard, but it might just change your life.

DISCUSSION QUESTIONS

1. Before the sabbatical, I had no regular time in God's Word or in prayer because of time constraints and responsibilities as a business owner, husband, and father. What obstacles stand in your way of spending focused time with God?

2. I had my reasons for not spending time in God's Word, but I certainly made time to watch sports, exercise, and relax. Are your answers above legitimate obstacles or are they excuses, like mine were, for not prioritizing time with God?

3. The circumstances of my life made me believe we had everything and our lives were perfect. What goals define your happiness, and are they a reflection of God's priorities?

4. What level of interaction do you have with the poor and hurting in your community?

5. What fears may keep you from opening up your life and home to people who are different than you?

6. I am asking you to pray the prayer that began this journey: *Lord, show me Your heart.* Be open to His message and ask Him to give you a fresh understanding of His specific call on your life to represent Him to a lost and broken world.

CHAPTER 2

GOD HAD A PLAN

God has given Meredith and me one of the most amazing gifts anyone could possibly receive: grandchildren. They are incredible! I'm not sure why I didn't enjoy being around children this much when our kids were young, but there is almost nothing I enjoy more than spending time with the grands. I guess I was at a different place in my life then, and to be perfectly honest, my priorities were seriously out of whack. But I have come to the conclusion that if we could go back and do things over, we would do our best to skip the kids and go straight to the grands.

As all three of our daughters have become adults, we have been blessed because they have remained close to home. This reality has allowed us to continue to spend time with them, but more importantly, it also means we get to spend time with the grands. We have four grandkids: Laura, Carter, Rissa and Reagan. A perfect day for me includes those four. I don't care if we are at the zoo, playing in the back yard, watching a kid's movie, or running errands. Our days are always better when we get to spend time with the grands.

Laura is our oldest. Laura and her mom (Amanda, our oldest daughter) lived with us for the first four years of Laura's life.

Meredith and I were able to be in the room when she was born, and I held her within seconds of her birth. Laura is nothing short of amazing. We have been right there with her as she has walked through the stages of life. We got to witness her rolling over, crawling, speaking, and taking steps for the first time.

Laura is smart as a whip and loves to learn. She has a thirst for knowledge and wants to share every new piece of information she learns with us. She wants to grow and do things for herself. While this desire is good, it can cause some frustration when she's not quite ready to pour her own cereal and it goes all over the kitchen floor, but have you ever wondered why kids want to become independent? Why do they have this inner desire to do things for themselves?

When Laura was three, she came into my office one night and announced, "Papa, we are going to work on our colors and letters." She walked over to a blank wall, pointed at it, and said, "Now what color is this, Papa?"

"Blue," I replied. The wall was actually cream, but I wanted to play along and see whatever object she was imagining.

"Very good," she said enthusiastically. "And what color is this?" She moved her finger a few inches to the left.

"Red," I replied.

"Very good, Papa." She then pointed to yet another area of the wall. "What letter is this, Papa?"

"I believe that is an *m*, Laura."

"Good job, Papa!"

This exchange continued for quite some time as we went through multiple colors and letters. A few days later we were driving down the road when she said, "Papa, look at me in the mirror. I have two eyeballs and guess what, Papa? You have two eyeballs too."

It was nice to hear her say I only had two eyeballs. I had often been referred to as "four eyes" during my childhood. It started in kindergarten and continued through most of my elementary school years, and I wasn't sure I wanted to go back to that painful time. The point is, Laura always wants to share some ground-breaking discovery with us. She is so proud of herself, and we make a big deal out of every new thing she does.

Watching my grandchildren grow and their thirst for knowledge and independence reminds me of one of the first things I learned during the sabbatical. That day in April 2002 when I read Genesis, it wasn't the first time I read the creation story. In fact, it wasn't even the first time I had read through the book of Genesis. I had failed many times at reading through the Bible, although I would always finish Genesis before February came and I abandoned my New Year's resolutions, but that day was different. My reading began with the same verses that most every "Read through the Bible" venture begins with.

> In the beginning God created the heavens and the earth. Now the earth was formless and empty, darkness covered the surface of the watery depths, and the Spirit of God was hovering over the surface of the waters. (Gen. 1:1-2)

The statement "The earth was formless and empty" brought up my first set of questions. For the first time, I thought about the fact that God had a completely blank canvas that He was working with. It was a clean slate. He could have made the world, and everything in it, any way He wanted to. Why did He create the things He created? Why did He create them to do what they do? Why did He say that what He created was good?

I did some research and found that the word translated as "good" in the Hebrew means that it was perfect. It was beautiful, better, or even best. He created exactly what He was trying to create, but I didn't understand why. As I continued to read through the creation story and into chapter 2, that's where things got interesting. I noticed something I'd never seen before.

This may not shock some of you, but it did me. I learned that God had a plan. He didn't randomly create things for no reason. God had a plan for how He would take care of humanity and how all of creation would work together within that plan for our good. Laura's desire to learn and grow is a perfect example of God's plan at work.

We see His plan played out in the life of every child. At a certain age they don't want us to take care of them anymore. They want to begin doing things independently. They want to care for themselves. Their desire is expressed through words that strike fear in the heart of every parent as they ring through their ears: *I wanna do it*. At that moment they take their stand and begin their journey towards independence.

For some reason, God created Adam with the need for a constant supply of food and water. It's important we remember that Adam was created with a need for these things. God could have created Adam with no needs whatsoever because, remember, He was working with a blank slate and He is God and could have done it however He wanted. For His creation to be considered "perfect," humans would die of thirst and starvation without food and water.

God provided for those needs through the garden. God also established a plan for Adam to meet those needs independently. We see God's plan introduced in Genesis 2. As soon as God created Adam, in verse seven, His plan was put into place. God's plan included three Fundamental Elements that are required for us to provide for our needs independently.

> *The LORD God planted a garden in Eden, in the east,*
> *and there He placed the man He had formed. The*
> *LORD God caused to grow out of the ground every*
> *tree pleasing in appearance and good for food,*

including the tree of life in the middle of the garden,
as well as the tree of the knowledge of good and evil.
A river went out from Eden to water the garden.
From there it divided and became the source of four
rivers. The name of the first is Pishon, which flows
through the entire land of Havilah, where there is
gold. Gold from that land is pure; bdellium and onyx
are also there. The name of the second river is Gihon,
which flows through the entire land of Cush. The
name of the third river is the Tigris, which runs east
of Assyria. And the fourth river the Euphrates. The
LORD God took the man and placed him in the
Garden of Eden to work it and watch over it. And the
LORD God commanded the man, "You are free to eat
from any tree of the garden, but you must not eat
from the tree of the knowledge of good and evil, for
on the day you eat from it, you will certainly die."
Then the LORD God said, "It is not good for the man
to be alone. I will make a helper as his complement."
(Gen. 2:8-18)

Adam had the need for food and water, and God provided those things in the garden. God planted the garden, which provided the necessary supplies to meet Adam's needs. The garden was full of trees and plants, and Adam had a natural desire for them. The garden had four rivers running through it to provide water. The garden provided Adam with the first Fundamental Element for Independence—*Resources.*

But Adam couldn't just walk into the garden and take the food. It was not Adam's garden. God created the garden and God put Adam there, but Adam didn't have permission to use the garden to meet his needs. Taking things that don't belong to you is called theft, which is a sin, and Adam was sinless at this point, so he needed permission. This brings us to the second Fundamental Element.

> And the LORD God commanded the man, "You are
> free to eat from any tree of the garden...." (Gen. 2:16)

Adam needed access to the resource and God gave it to him. He had gained the second Fundamental Element—*Opportunity*.

Here is where it gets interesting. Before God gave Adam the opportunity to use the garden, He put a requirement on him. Adam had to do something if he was going to gain the resources that were available in the garden.

> The LORD God took the man and placed him in the
> Garden of Eden to work it and watch over it.
> (Gen. 2:15)

God placed Adam right in middle of the resource, but it wasn't free. Adam had to work for it. God gave Adam a job. God's perfect creation and plan would include a requirement of Adam. He was given the responsibility to work and watch over the garden.

Adam had to work, but God, being the God that He is, provided for Adam's need. He didn't just tell Adam to, "Go to work." He didn't tell Adam to, "Figure it out." He didn't leave Adam alone. God gave Adam the information he needed to know.

Most companies have an employee manual. This manual defines the expectations, policies, and procedures for getting things done. Employees read the manual (or least they sign a document saying that they have read it) to gain an understanding of the company's culture. They need to know the rules. God gave Adam the rules of the garden.

> And the LORD God commanded the man, "You are
> free to eat from any tree of the garden, but you must
> not eat from the tree of the knowledge of good and

evil, for on the day you eat from it, you will certainly die." (Gen. 2:16-17)

Adam needed to know the rules. He needed to have the specific dos and don'ts of the garden. God had established boundaries for the garden, and Adam needed to know what those boundaries were. Verses 16 and 17 record the first ever employee manual, but is knowledge of the rules all we need? This got me thinking, and I began to read the section again. That's when I noticed something that required a little more study.

> *The LORD God planted a garden in Eden, in the east, and there He placed the man He had formed.* (Gen. 2:8)

In the creation story, in Genesis 1, the Bible says, "God created" certain things and, "God said" for other things to come into existence. *"God created the heavens and the earth." "God said let there be light." "God said let there be an expanse between the waters." "God created man in His own image."* God created things or He spoke and it happened, but that changed in chapter 2. God didn't create the garden and He didn't speak it into existence. Verse 8 says He "planted" it.

This seemed significant, so I did some studying and found that the Hebrew word for "planted" is *nâṭa'* (pronounced *naw-tah'*). This is a literal word. It is the same word that is used other places in the Old Testament when it is recorded that a person has or was told to plant a garden or a vineyard. This is a literal word that carries some interesting implications. The use of this word changed my understanding of God in the garden.

I had always pictured God continuing to create the way He did in Genesis 1. God snapped His fingers and said, "Let there be a garden" and *poof*, the garden appeared. The use of the word *nâṭa'* means that God actually did the work. This means that God, the almighty, infinite, Creator got down on His hands and knees and literally tore up the dirt and placed the seeds in the ground. When I talked with an Old Testament professor about this, he said, "You're exactly right. Our God got dirt under His fingernails."

While I thought this was a cool piece of information, it brought up a question. Why? Why would God, the awesome Creator of everything, the all-powerful master of the universe, do this work? Why would He get on the ground and get His hands dirty planting a garden? All He had to do was say a word and it would exist, but that's not what God did. For some reason, the planting of the garden was part of His perfect plan.

After spending some time meditating on this, it hit me. God used the garden as a training facility. He used it to teach Adam how to work the ground and plant the seeds. Adam needed the knowledge and God was his personal instructor. As the teacher, God gave Adam a lesson in gardening. God gave Adam the rules and God provided "hands-on" training. God gave Adam both parts of the third Fundamental Element he needed to be independent—*Instruction*.

This new understanding of the Three Fundamental Elements for self-sufficiency caused me to change the way I think. I'm sure you've heard the old saying about the importance of teaching and not just giving something to someone. The saying goes like this: *"Give a man a fish and you feed him for a day. Teach a man to fish and you'll feed him for a lifetime."*

I had repeated that saying for years, until I began to understand the real needs of people and the Fundamental Elements God had provided in His plan. This new understanding taught me that giving instruction alone is not enough. If you don't live anywhere near water, don't have any equipment, or don't have permission to use any of it, you're in bad shape. Knowing "how to" fish won't feed your family without the other elements. You must have Resources and Opportunity as well as Instruction.

These three Fundamental Elements provide everything needed to live. While you can get by with resources, opportunity, and instruction, is that all there is to God's plan? Did God just want us to "get by"? Isn't there more to life than just making a living? Once again, we can look to my grandkids for help. (Have I mentioned how much I enjoy being around them?)

One of my favorite "Laura" stories happened just before her fourth birthday. Every night, Nana or Mom would give Laura a bath. On this particular evening Laura announced she had come to the decision she was no longer in need of assistance while getting ready for bed. This would be the night that she was going to do it all by herself. Nana and Mom would not be in the room to supervise. We were nervous, but she knew she could do it and she wanted the opportunity to handle it on her own.

We had given her two of the three Fundamental Elements. She had the resources (tub, soap, shampoo, and jammies). She had received both sides of the instruction, Mom and Nana had taught her how to get ready for bed by herself, and she knew the water was supposed to stay inside the tub. The only Element she was missing was the opportunity. No matter how nervous we were about her being in the bathroom all alone, she was getting her chance to do it on her own.

I went to my office, which is next to the bathroom, and Meredith and Amanda went downstairs. Laura had never been in a tub full of water unsupervised, so every couple of minutes I knocked on the door to check on her. "Laura, are you OK?" I would ask through the door. "Yes, Papa. I'm taking my bath," she would respond. I could tell by the sound in her voice she was getting tired of my checking on her after the first couple of times. About fifteen minutes later she came walking out of the bathroom completely ready for bed. She came into my office and said, "Papa, look. I took my bath and got my jammies on all by myself. Aren't you so very proud of me?"

29

"Yes, I am, Laura," I said.

"Do you wan' a hug?" she asked.

"Yes, I do."

She came over and gave me a big hug and a kiss and proceeded downstairs into the room where Meredith was reading. I heard her proud little voice.

"Nana, look. I took my bath and got my jammies on all by myself. Aren't you so very proud of me?"

"Yes," Meredith said.

"Do you wan' a hug?"

I heard her move to the next room of the house and begin the conversation again with "Mama, look." Laura went to every single person in the house that night. She repeated the same lines to all of us. I smiled as I listened to her tell the exact same story of her accomplishments four different times. I realized that her desire to be independent, her pride in herself, and her need to share it were all part of God's plan. They were all part of the plan that He deemed perfect.

Laura sharing her success reminded me that God gave Adam a fourth Fundamental Element. Adam was given everything he needed to live, but just living wasn't enough. God wanted more for Adam and He wants more for us. I've learned that there is a difference between living and having a life. God wants us to have life and have it more abundantly. The ability to merely meet our needs is not what God planned for humanity.

Let's go back to the creation story. The record of God's creation is not written in chronological order. Chapter 2 of Genesis takes place as a part of the creation story in chapter 1. Chapter 1 references the time line of when it happened, but chapter 2 gives the specifics and tells us why it happened. Let's put the two passages together to better understand the importance of the fourth Fundamental Element.

After each step of creation in chapter 1, God said that "it was good." The only exception was day two, where it is not recorded that God said this. Since Saturday was the original Sabbath, Sunday would have been the first day of the week. God's silence on day two shows us that God does not like Mondays either, but here is what He did say: Day 1, light—"It was good." Day 2, earth and sky—silence. Day 3, vegetation—"It was good." Day 4, sun, moon, and stars—"It was good." Day 5, the fish and the birds—"It was good." Stop. This is where chapter 2 has to be inserted into the time line. Day six is broken into two parts. God created Adam and then this happened.

> Then the LORD God said, "It is not good for the man to be alone. I will make a helper as his complement." So the LORD God formed out of the ground every wild animal and every bird of the sky, and brought each to the man to see what he would call it. And whatever the man called a living creature, that was its name. The man gave names to all the livestock, to the birds of the sky, and to every wild animal; but for the man no helper was found as his complement. So the LORD God caused a deep sleep to come over the man, and he slept. God took one of his ribs and closed the flesh at that place. Then the LORD God made the rib He had taken from the man into a woman and brought her to the man. (Gen. 2:18-22)

Genesis 1 tells us that after God made the animals on day six, He called that creation good, but do you see what God said about the man being alone? It is the only part of creation that God said was "not good." Every animal had been made in pairs, but the man was going to be alone. God knew that this would not provide Adam with what he needed to have a full life. He needed "a helper as his complement."

31

Now let me chase a rabbit here because this is too important to pass by. God did not make a servant who would blindly obey Adam's instructions and wait on his every whim. Adam needed a "complement" because his isolation was "not good." Adam needed someone he could come home to at night and say, "Look what I've done. Aren't you so very proud of me? Do you want a hug?" Adam needed more than just to live—he needed a partner with whom he could share his life. I think one of the most damaging things we have done in our culture is to reduce women to the role of a mere "helper." That is not what God intended for Adam and Eve.

The word "helper" in Hebrew is *'ēzer* (pronounced *ay'-zer)*. It is not a subordinate. It's not an assistant who is beneath the leader. God used a very powerful word that we translate as "helper." The word is used to show a supporter, a necessity, even a rescuer. An *'ēzer* is something you cannot do without.

The Hebrew word is used twenty-two times in the Old Testament. Only six times is it used in reference to a human. Three of those times are here in Genesis 2, and the other three times, it says that people will fail as our helper. The remaining sixteen times this word is used, it refers to God. It shows God as the only source of help in a time of trouble, the only one who can be relied upon. It shows God as the source of our supply. David uses this word ten times in the book of Psalms as an understanding that God is his provider.

> *A song of ascents. I lift my eyes toward the mountains. Where will my help come from? My help comes from the LORD, the Maker of heaven and earth.* (Ps. 121:1-2)

David was desperate and lacking. He had to be rescued. That is the same word for "helper" in Genesis 2. Now why is this so important? Because God knew that Adam's life was incomplete.

Adam was missing something very important. Adam needed someone to share his life with, someone to support and encourage him in times of trouble, and someone to laugh and celebrate with when times were good. God knew the importance of having someone whom Adam could rely upon as his "helper." What Adam was missing was a connection. God knew Adam's life could not be complete without fellowship.

Relationships are the final element and, by far, the most important of the Four Fundamental Elements. Relationships are so important to having a healthy life that the lack of them can have catastrophic effects. The opposite of relationships is isolation. Studies have shown that isolation causes a higher rate of heart disease and can even cause insanity.[1] When someone is in prison and they egregiously break the rules, how are they punished? They are put in solitary confinement and separated from others. Isolating someone is the worst form of punishment.

Children who did not receive relational interaction during their formative years experienced debilitating effects. A study of children living in Russian orphanages in the 1940s showed that those who were given the proper food and water, but lacked physical interaction with others, had a higher rate of infections and were developmentally behind other children.[2] God created us in such a way that our physical, mental, and emotional health depends upon relationships. God created us with a deep need for them. The Bible is filled with stories highlighting the importance of relationships.

Abraham was tested with the life of his son Isaac. The highest test Abraham could pass was offering his son as a sacrifice. God provided and the promised heir was saved. How did God introduce Himself when He met Moses on Mt Sinai and wanted him to go back to Egypt and lead the people out of slavery? He told Moses to stay back, and then He made His introduction:

Then He continued, "I am the God of your father, the God of Abraham, the God of Isaac, and the God of Jacob." Moses hid his face because he was afraid to look at God. (Exod. 3:6)

God let Moses know that He was the God of his family. He was the God who had made covenants. He was the God of miracles. He could be trusted. He was their God and would bring them out of slavery. The relational aspect continues through this story when Moses came before Pharaoh. Moses told Pharaoh to let the people go, and how did Pharaoh respond?

"Who is Yahweh that I should obey Him by letting Israel go? I do not know anything about Yahweh, and besides, I will not let Israel go." (Exod. 5:2)

I've always known that Pharaoh didn't worship God. Then I realized that Pharaoh would not let the people go because he did not know who God was. Remember, Pharaoh thought that he himself was a god. He didn't need to bow down to some unknown deity his slaves worshipped. Pharaoh's downfall and the destruction of the entire Egyptian army came about because Pharaoh did not have a relationship with God.

All of the Ten Commandments are based upon relationships. The first four talk about our relationship with God. The last six talk about our relationship with others. The law that was recorded in Leviticus lays out guideline after guideline about how we are supposed to relate to each other. Relationships are the entire subject of Scripture from Genesis to Revelation.

In the beginning God had a perfect relationship with Himself. In the garden He had a perfect relationship with Adam and Eve. When sin entered the world, that relationship was broken. The rest of Scripture, from beginning to end, records God reaching out to reestablish relationships with humanity. In the end, we will have a perfect relationship with Him again. Proper relationships are the basis of God's plan.

Back to the creation story. God knew it was "not good" for Adam to be alone. God knew that for Adam's well-being, he would need to have a mate. He could not have a full life without one. God created His plan to meet Adam's needs perfectly. For us to be healthy and have that same full life, we must have relationships with others. What did God think when He finished His work and looked at His completed creation?

> *God saw all that He had made, and it was very good.*
> *Evening came and then morning: the sixth day.*
> (Gen. 1:31)

God's creation was perfect until He created a partner for Adam. This creation allowed Adam to no longer be alone, but to be in relationship with others who were like him. God looked at the final step of His creation, and it was even better than perfect. It was exponentially perfect. With the addition of relationships God said it was "very good." Creation was complete, God's plan was in place, and it was perfectly perfect.

DISCUSSION QUESTIONS

1. What is the first memory you have of someone refusing help because they wanted to independently overcome a challenge and do it for themselves?
2. Why is it important for us to understand that God created us to take care of ourselves?
3. Write a list of resources that would be necessary for someone to be self-sufficient.
4. What are some examples of opportunities that you were given to take on responsibility and care for yourself?
5. How does the understanding of God planting the garden change your thoughts on God?
6. God created us to be in relationships. Who do you have in your life that encourages, supports, and challenges you to be the best version of you? If you don't have someone, please seek that support system.

CHAPTER 3

GOD'S PLAN IN THE OLD TESTAMENT

Have you ever been deeply hurt by someone you love? Have you ever felt the sting when you realize you've been lied to? I remember the first time I caught Laura lying to me. We were in the den, and she was playing with a sticker book on the coffee table, and I was sitting on the couch working on this book. We both had a cup of coffee. Laura loves having "coffee" with Nana and Papa, which is actually 95 percent milk and 5 percent coffee, she loves to make the *ahhhhh* sound after each sip.

We were having a great morning enjoying being in the same room together while we did our "work." I noticed Laura get up and leave the room, but I didn't think much of it because she is a pretty independent child. A few minutes later I realized that she had not come back, so I called her name, but she didn't respond. Then I called a second time, this time a little louder, in case she was upstairs and didn't hear me. I still heard no response, so I got up to see where she was.

I walked through the kitchen and into the dining room and didn't see her. I went through the sitting area and checked the downstairs bathroom. No Laura. I went upstairs and looked through the bedrooms, office, and bathrooms and still no Laura.

Starting to get a little concerned, I came back downstairs and called her name again. I heard a quiet voice from the dining room answer, "Yes, Papa." I walked in there, but still didn't see her.

I called again and heard from under the table, "Yes, Papa." I crouched down and there was Laura. She was sitting under the middle of the table with all the chairs pulled in. There she was, in all her glory, with the remains of a chocolate chip cookie on her face. There was a plate of cookies in the kitchen, so I asked if she had gotten into the cookies. She said no.

I wasn't upset. In fact, I thought it was pretty funny, but it did bother me. I had just caught someone that I had been able to trust completely, and one of the most precious people in the world to me, in a lie. My confidence in her ability to tell me the truth was shaken. I recently read a version of a quote by Friedrich Nietzsche that explained my emotion in that moment. *"I'm not upset that you lied to me, I'm upset that from now on I can't believe you."* [1]

This happened to God. His creation was complete and His plan was "perfectly perfect." Adam and Eve would work to provide for their own needs, but satan had a different plan (and yes, the word *satan* is not capitalized on purpose. I refuse to give him that dignity). When satan wanted to throw a wrench into God's perfect plan, his first attack was to bring doubt on God's word.

Why would this be satan's first line of attack? Why call God's honesty and integrity into question? I believe it's because he knew that trust is the basis of every relationship, and that relationships were the most important thing God had given Adam and Eve. satan knew that if you don't have trust, then the relationship is bound to suffer. The goal of the deceiver was to break the relationship.

Adam and Eve took satan's bait and sinned. Notice the immediate change in their relationships.

> *Then the man and his wife heard the sound of the*
> *LORD God walking in the garden at the time of the*

38

evening breeze, and they hid themselves from the LORD God among the trees of the garden. So the LORD God called out to the man and said to him, "Where are you?" And he said, "I heard You in the garden and I was afraid because I was naked, so I hid." Then He asked, "Who told you that you were naked? Did you eat from the tree that I commanded you not to eat from?" Then the man replied, "The woman You gave to be with me—she gave me some fruit from the tree, and I ate." (Gen. 3:8-12)

As soon as Adam and Eve sinned, their relationship with each other and with God changed. They had welcomed God and walked with God and now they hid. They hid under the table with all the chairs pulled in. The relationship that had been built on trust had been shattered by fear. The result of sin on the relationships is seen when Adam blamed God and Eve for his own sin. The trust was gone and God's perfect creation was damaged.

Sin entered the world and Adam began to operate out of selfish motives. In fact, I think selfishness may be the most succinct definition of sin. God, at that moment, had a window of opportunity. He could change anything, He could change everything, or He could change nothing at all. With all the things that changed, God didn't change His plan.

He removed Adam and Eve from the garden and suddenly their lives would be harder. Because of their rebellion, more work would be required for them to gain an even smaller yield. Their pain and suffering increased. Death entered the world, but the plan remained. They would still be responsible to work to provide for their own needs, and God's plan is continually seen throughout the rest of Scripture.

In Genesis 6, we read that mankind had grown wicked and all their schemes were evil all the time. God was fed up. He decided He was going to destroy all living things from the face of the earth.

He was going to wipe the plate clean and start over, but not completely. There was one man God would save.

> *But Noah found favor in the eyes of the LORD. These are the family records of Noah. Noah was a righteous man, blameless among his contemporaries; Noah walked with God.* (Gen. 6:8-9)

God would start over with Noah, but how would He do it? He flooded the entire earth and destroyed every living thing, but saved Noah and his family. God could have made it easy on Noah. He could have had Noah go into the woods, where he would find a big boat that was filled with all the food and supplies he would need. The boat would have been completely ready to go. All Noah would need to do is load up and ride out the storm.

God could have had all the tools drop-shipped to Noah's front porch. He could have had the materials delivered to the side yard. That's the way it happened in the Hollywood comedy, but that is not what God did. God worked within the plan He had established in the garden. Noah had to do the work himself.

Not only did Noah do the work, he may have had to make his own tools. There is no record of Noah running to the hardware store to pick up a saw, some pitch, and a lift to put the logs in place and hold them all together. He would have had to cut down the trees and manually move them into place. Then he would have had to shape the lumber and maneuver it. All this was done by hand with no power tools or a hydraulic crane. Noah had to move large logs 45 feet into the air, without the use of modern machinery. I think we can all agree that this was not an easy task. It took him 120 years to finish the ark, but even so, God provided the Four Fundamental Elements.

> *Then God said to Noah, "I have decided to put an end to all flesh, for the earth is filled with violence because of them; therefore I am going to destroy*

them along with the earth. Make yourself an ark of gofer wood. Make rooms in the ark, and cover it with pitch inside and outside. This is how you are to make it: The ark will be 450 feet long, 75 feet wide, and 45 feet high. You are to make a roof, finishing the sides of the ark to within 18 inches of the roof. You are to put a door in the side of the ark. Make it with lower, middle, and upper decks. Understand that I am bringing a deluge—floodwaters on the earth to destroy all flesh under heaven with the breath of life in it. Everything on earth will die. But I will establish My covenant with you, and you will enter the ark with your sons, your wife, and your sons' wives. You are also to bring into the ark two of every living thing of all flesh, male and female, to keep them alive with you. Two of everything—from the birds according to their kinds, from the livestock according to their kinds, and from every animal that crawls on the ground according to its kind—will come to you so that you can keep them alive. Take with you every kind of food that is eaten; gather it as food for you and for them." (Gen. 6:13-21)

Noah needed the resources to build the ark. He had to have the supplies. There is no record of how God provided these resources, but apparently they were available in that region, and Noah obviously got them. I think it's safe to say they would have existed in the surrounding area, because it is clear that Noah had the materials to do the work. God provided the resources.

God could have impressed it on Noah's heart and made him do the work. Noah would have responded in a robotic fashion and the ark would have been built, but instead, God presented Noah with the chance to build the ark. It wasn't forced on him. I have often wondered what would have happened if Noah had said no, but he didn't. He was given a choice and, with that choice, God gave Noah an opportunity.

God also provided all the information Noah needed. He told him why He was going to destroy the world, how He was going to destroy the world, and how He was going to save Noah and his family. He gave Noah the specific instructions on how to build the ark and what to take for food. There were no questions left. God had given Noah instruction. All Noah had to do was the work.

But God knew that Noah could not do this alone. What kind of life would Noah have if he were stuck on a boat, for months on end all by himself, and how would he repopulate the earth? God deepened His own relationship with Noah when He established a covenant, but He allowed Noah's wife, sons, and daughters-in-law to be included. God had already established that it is not good for a man to be alone and none of the animals were suitable mates. God gave Noah relationships with Himself, through the covenant, as well as with his wife and children.

God used His plan to save Noah, his family, and all the animals. The resources were made available, the opportunity was extended, Noah was given specific instructions, and relationships were included. Noah could save humanity, but he would have to work for it. God told Noah to do the work. He didn't do it for him.

I want you to notice something interesting about God's plan. God made Noah do everything that was within his power to accomplish. The only thing God provided for Noah was something that was outside of Noah's ability. God brought the animals to the ark. Noah did everything else. This is the same pattern God used with Adam. Adam had the abilities to do the work, and God only provided what he was unable to provide for himself.

God's plan is also used in Exodus, when He called the people of Israel to build a place for His presence to dwell among them. He could have had the people come to a specific spot in the desert, or He could have had them meet Him on the mountain, like He did in Exodus 19, but that was no longer what God wanted. He wanted a permanent place. God wanted them to build a sanctuary, and He stuck with His plan to have the men of Israel do the work through the Four Fundamental Elements. The record of the provision of resources is in Exodus 25.

> *"Tell the Israelites to take an offering for Me. You are*
> *to take My offering from everyone whose heart stirs*
> *him to give...."* (Exod. 25:2)

The next few verses list the items they were to bring. God also gave them the opportunity and commanded them to do the work.

> *"They are to make a sanctuary for Me so that I may*
> *dwell among them...."* (Exod. 25:8)

God provided detailed instructions about how the sanctuary was to be built, as well as everything that was to be used in it for worship. Here are just a couple of the verses as an example.

> *"They are to make an ark of acacia wood, 45 inches*
> *long, 27 inches wide, and 27 inches high. Overlay it*
> *with pure gold; overlay it inside and out. Also make*
> *a gold molding all around it...."* (Exod. 25:10-11)

God gave very specific instructions concerning exactly how to build every aspect of the sanctuary. He determined the size, shape, color, and materials. God even gave instructions on how every item, which would be used in worship, was to be made. The above example is the beginning of the design for the Ark of the Covenant, which God provided a total of eighteen verses of instruction. God didn't leave any question unanswered concerning the design and layout of the sanctuary and all of its furnishings. He gave precise details. Chapter 25 ends with the following instruction:

> *"Be careful to make them according to the pattern*
> *you have been shown...."* (Exod. 25:40)

God also provided relationships as they built the sanctuary.

> *Look, I have appointed by name Bezalel son of Uri,*
> *son of Hur, of the tribe of Judah. I have filled him with*
> *God's Spirit, with wisdom, understanding, and ability*
> *in every craft to design artistic works in gold, silver,*
> *and bronze, to cut gemstones for mounting, and to*
> *carve wood for work in every craft. I have also*
> *selected Oholiab son of Ahisamach, of the tribe of*
> *Dan, to be with him. I have placed wisdom within*
> *every skilled craftsman in order to make all that I*
> *have commanded you: the tent of meeting, the ark of*
> *the testimony, the mercy seat that is on top of it, and*
> *all the other furnishings of the tent....* (Exod. 31:2-7)

God made available all four Fundamental Elements so the Israelites could be successful in fulfilling His commands. He gave the resources, the opportunity, the instruction, and the relationships. Just like He did with Adam and Noah, we see the only thing God provided was something outside of human abilities. In this case, it was His presence. Every other part was done by the men of Israel. God created the plan, God implemented the plan, and God stuck with the plan.

Many other places in the Old Testament illustrate God's plan, but let's look at one more section before we move on. The Ten Commandments. The Ten Commandments show us God's plan. As we saw in the last chapter, they certainly involve relationships. The first four concern our relationship with God and the last six cover our relationship with others, but do they say anything about work?

Now, I don't know about your experience growing up, but the fourth commandment was a pretty big deal around our house. During my childhood, I cannot remember a single Sunday when we went out to eat. When I asked about it I was told, "We don't go out to eat because we want to honor the Sabbath and by going out to eat, we would require someone else to work." While I admired that commitment to our beliefs, I did notice this didn't seem to equally apply to watching sports; which required the work of the players, refs, and broadcast teams. Regardless, Sunday was always a special day of rest in the Kendall household.

Remember the Sabbath, to keep it holy: (Exod. 20:8)

Have you ever thought about the fact that there is another side of the fourth commandment? It doesn't end in verse eight. It continues into verse 9.

> *You are to labor six days and do all your work, but the seventh day is a Sabbath to the LORD your God. You must not do any work—you, your son or daughter, your male or female slave, your livestock, or the foreigner who is within your gates. For the LORD made the heavens and the earth, the sea, and everything in them in six days; then He rested on the seventh day. Therefore the LORD blessed the Sabbath day and declared it holy.* (Exod. 20:9-11)

Verse 9 begins with a command. "You are to labor six days." It doesn't say, "If you labor." It is a direct command to work. While I learned the importance of resting on the Sabbath, I have to wonder if the second part of the command was for others who were not taught to work. It is just as important for us to understand the command to work the other six days as it is to rest on the seventh. To put an emphasis on the one and ignore the other is hypocritical.

This call to work and rest was so important that God used Himself as an example. The fourth commandment is unique. While God gives further instructions or deeper understanding in the second, third, and fifth commandments, the fourth commandment is the only one where He uses Himself as the standard. He did all the work of creation in six days and then He rested. We are to follow His example.

In Exodus 34, Moses was called to the top of Mount Sanai because God was going to give him a second set of the Ten Commandments, because the first set was destroyed. In this chapter, God gave Moses a lot of additional instructions concerning the children of Israel, but He also mentioned two of the commandments specifically. The first one mentioned is the second commandment, which instructed them not to build or worship any images. God protected their relationship. The other commandment mentioned is the fourth commandment, to work for six days and rest on the seventh. God was not messing around with His plan for people to work to provide for their own needs.

We are instructed to work. It's not an option, it's not a choice—it is a command. While presenting this material I have had people ask if there are any examples in Scripture of someone not using God's plan. As a matter of fact, there is more than one.

Most of us have heard of King David, who would be a Hollywood star if he were alive today. He was a man of action. He was a man's man. He was good looking and tough. He killed the giant Goliath. He killed a bear and a lion with his bare hands. He could live in a cave and fight with the best of them. He is spoken of like a hero in Scripture.

He was also a man who displayed incredible character for most of his life. He was chosen by God as the king of Israel. He had a quick mind, showed compassion, and had integrity. He displayed mercy towards his political enemies and always respected the people whom God had put in places of authority, even if they wanted to kill him. David was the total package. He was the real deal, but with all the accolades of King David, he wasn't perfect. David made some major mistakes in his life. Here are the high points of David's most famous failures.

- He saw Bathsheba (a married woman) bathing and had her brought to the palace.
- He slept with her and got her pregnant.
- David found out she was pregnant and summoned Uriah (Bathsheba's husband) home from the war.
- David sent Uriah home to sleep with his wife, but Uriah was a man of integrity and would not sleep with his wife while the ark of the covenant, Israel, and Judah were sleeping in tents and out to war.
- David was a little frustrated and had Uriah stay another day and got him drunk and sent him home to his wife, but once again, Uriah displayed incredible character and integrity. Even while drunk, Uriah had enough sense about him that he chose to sleep on the steps of the castle.
- Uriah had proven himself to David. He was a man who could be trusted, so David gave a written message for Uriah to deliver back to the front lines.
- Uriah, being a man of integrity, didn't open the letter from the King, which contained the plan to retreat in the heat of the battle, leaving Uriah alone on the front line to be killed.

Adultery, deception, and murder. These are the new attributes of King David. I am amazed that even after all this, it is recorded that David was *"A man after [God's] own heart"* (Acts 13:22 NIV). To this day, people want to name their sons after King David, the hero of Scripture, and not Uriah, the one who displayed character and integrity during the entire situation. Although I think it would be tough growing up with a name like Uriah. So, what does all this have to do with God's plan for people to work? The answer is found in 2 Samuel 11.

> *In the spring when kings march out to war, David sent Joab with his officers and all Israel. They*

destroyed the Ammonites and besieged Rabbah, but
David remained in Jerusalem. (2 Sam. 11:1)

Do you see it? Do you see how this fits into God's plan? David did not go to work. He did not show up and do his job. It was the King's job to lead his men out to war. That was the pattern David had displayed in his life. Fifteen times in 2 Samuel chapters 1-10, it is recorded that David led the army out to war, but on this occasion David decided to skip work and stay home. The very next verse is where David gets into trouble.

One evening David got up from his bed and strolled around on the roof of the palace. From the roof he saw a woman bathing—a very beautiful woman. (2 Sam. 11:2)

David was sitting at home when he should have been at work. His legacy was changed because he did not do his job. David's downfall was that he was not fulfilling his role in God's plan. David not only skipped work, but he left himself isolated from the most important Fundamental Element—Relationships. He sent his closest advisors out to war. Joab was not only his General, but he was his nephew and his right-hand man. The men he had fought and bled with were sent away, and David was left alone with no one to hold him accountable.

David's choice to stay at home, when he should have been at work, changed his entire legacy. His new legacy included a lot of things for which none of us would want to be remembered. I have to wonder how this incident would have ended differently had one of David's men, one of the men who could have held David accountable, had been in Jerusalem with him. David's children suffered from their father's choices and they followed in his footsteps. They also chose lust, adultery, deception, and murder. David is a perfect example of what happens when people do not follow God's plan.

God established the plan in the garden and put it into place. He used it with Noah. He used it with the children of Israel. He speaks specifically to it in the Ten Commandments, and we have seen what happens when we don't follow His plan. God designed us to care for our own needs, and He commands us to work as a means to fulfill those needs.

Now I have presented this material enough to know that I am about to lose some of you. While some of you are shouting amen, others are getting frustrated and are ready to put this book down. I can appreciate the desire to walk away when presented with something new, and this understanding of God's plan is new to many of you. Those who are ready to walk away often tell me that I am just trying to support my political opinions with this book.

While this may sound like a political platform at some levels, I can assure you I am not trying to promote any one political party over the other. I have very little faith in the Republicans or the Democrats to do what is right in God's eyes, and our government's track record for ending poverty is unimpressive, regardless of who is in office. The war between the US government and poverty is over, and poverty has won. I am simply sharing what I learned when I asked God to show me His heart. Nothing more, nothing less.

While I don't trust our government to end poverty, I do have faith in God. I have faith that He can and will finish what He has started. I have faith that He loves us and wants what is best for us. I have faith that His love for humanity includes the poor. He loves the poor and He wants what is best for the poor. I have faith that He knows what He is doing. He has a plan to restore the poor, and it is not our job to question Him, but to live within His plan and follow it.

DISCUSSION QUESTIONS

1. Describe the situation and how you felt the first time you found out that someone you trusted had lied to you.
2. How does satan attack relationships today?
3. How has social media improved or damaged our abilities to have deep, lasting relationships?
4. What do you think God would have done if Noah had said no and refused to build the ark?
5. How do we lovingly communicate God's command for us to work six days a week to people who haven't grown up with this understanding?
6. How would David's life have been different if he had not sent his closest companions away?
7. Do you have people who hold you accountable?

CHAPTER 4

GOD'S PLAN IN THE NEW TESTAMENT

A second concern I have heard from people who struggle with God's plan is that I am legalistic: *Rob, that's all Old Testament stuff. We're a New Testament church. The New Testament is about grace, mercy, and love. The New Testament calls us to care for the least of these.*

They're right. A lot of things did change in the New Testament. The New Testament is about grace, mercy, and love. Matthew 25 does call us to care for the "least of these," but what does that mean? Does the New Testament say anything about God's plan? To better understand this we need to put life and society into perspective for the time period that the New Testament was written.

What would the original audience have understood when they heard what Jesus, or any of His followers, said about work? How would their life experience be different from ours? How would their understanding of society have filtered the words that were spoken? I've heard it said that I don't see things the way they are, but the way I am. We have to see things through the eyes of the New Testament audience to really understand the meaning of what was taught.

In New Testament times, people had to work hard to take care of their families. Most societies were agrarian, which means people grew their own food, raised their own cattle, and did not have easy access to water. In fact, they would have been required to walk to a well in the center of town, fill large cisterns with water, and carry the heavy pots back to their homes. Marketplaces were uncommon in less populated areas, and much of the business was done through a barter system. We need to remember this as we put the New Testament into perspective. They understood that hard work was a common and important part of everyday life. Hard work was necessary to live.

Paul wrote more than half of the New Testament, so let's look at what he has to say about God's plan. Paul was a guy who liked to put his money where his mouth was—and he worked. After leaving his comfortable position as a Pharisee, he became a tentmaker. Paul's example of working to care for his own needs was well known. His commitment to work was so well known it is referred to as a "tradition" which others were familiar with in 2 Thessalonians 3:6. The references to him working are found in several areas of Scripture. It is recorded that Paul worked to support his own needs in Ephesus, Corinth, and Thessalonica.

As Paul was leaving the church at Ephesus, after ministering there for two years, he had this to say to the elders:

> "I have not coveted anyone's silver or gold or clothing. You yourselves know that these hands have provided for my needs and for those who were with me." (Acts 20:33-34)

Now I am not trying to make the case that people involved in ministry should not gain their incomes from their work. When Paul was writing to Timothy on the subject of paid ministers, he quoted the words of Jesus, recorded in both Matthew 10:10

and Luke 10:7 concerning the workers being worthy of their pay. Paul says the same thing in 1 Timothy concerning elders.

> *The elders who are good leaders should be considered worthy of an ample honorarium, especially those who work hard at preaching and teaching. For the Scripture says: Do not muzzle an ox while it is treading out the grain, and, the worker is worthy of his wages.* (1 Tim. 5:17-18)

Paul addresses this same issue in 1 Corinthians 9 by saying he and Barnabas had the right to be supported by the work they did. In 1 Corinthians 16, Paul says the gifts that were brought to them refreshed his spirit. So Paul did accept money for his work at times, but he also used himself up as an example of working hard to provide for his own needs. When teaching in a town, he often refused this right of support for the sake of the gospel, but the point is that we know Paul worked on a regular basis.

Paul also commanded those who traveled with him to work to provide for their own needs. He would not allow his companions to eat the bread of someone else without paying for it.

> *It is not that we don't have the right to support, but we did it to make ourselves an example to you so that you would imitate us. In fact, when we were with you, this is what we commanded you: "If anyone isn't willing to work, he should not eat."* (2 Thess. 3:9-10)

On at least four other occasions, Paul called people to work to provide for their own needs.

> *The thief must no longer steal. Instead, he must do honest work with his own hands, so that he has something to share with anyone in need.* (Eph. 4:28)

> *Slaves, obey your human masters with fear and trembling, in the sincerity of your heart, as to Christ.*

Don't work only while being watched, in order to please men, but as slaves of Christ, do God's will from your heart. Serve with a good attitude, as to the Lord and not to men, knowing that whatever good each one does, slave or free, he will receive this back from the Lord. (Eph. 6:5-8)

Slaves, obey your human masters in everything. Don't work only while being watched, in order to please men, but work wholeheartedly, fearing the Lord. (Col. 3:22)

About brotherly love: you don't need me to write you because you yourselves are taught by God to love one another. In fact, you are doing this toward all the brothers in the entire region of Macedonia. But we encourage you, brothers, to do so even more, to seek to lead a quiet life, to mind your own business, and to work with your own hands, as we commanded you, so that you may walk properly in the presence of outsiders and not be dependent on anyone. (1 Thess. 4:9-12)

Paul consistently taught that working to provide for your own needs is something people should do. He did it himself and required it out of those who were with him. He goes even further to say that working hard is one of the attributes of followers of Christ. In the Ephesians 6 passage, above, he says it is "God's will" that we should work. Paul makes it very clear we should work and that our work is done for the Lord and not to please others.

The last passage above (1 Thess. 4) is amazing because Paul takes working to provide for your own needs to an even deeper level. He tells them that they are showing love already, but they should show love "even more." How is this love shown? By "leading a quiet life, minding your own business, and working with your own hands." This is not a suggestion. Paul says he has "commanded" them to do this. He ends by saying that this is considered "walking properly." Paul supports God's system and expects people to work.

Now if leading a quiet life, minding your own business, and working with your own hands is considered brotherly love, then those who don't do these things are not loving their brothers. Not leading a quiet life, not minding your own business, and not working with your own hands displays hatred and it means you are not walking properly. That may sound harsh, but that is exactly what Paul is teaching. Just in case there was some question about Paul's position, he makes this very clear in his second letter to the Thessalonians.

> *Now we command you, brothers, in the name of our Lord Jesus Christ, to keep away from every brother who walks irresponsibly and not according to the tradition received from us. For you yourselves know how you must imitate us: we were not irresponsible among you; we did not eat anyone's bread free of charge; instead, we labored and struggled, working night and day, so that we would not be a burden to any of you. It is not that we don't have the right to support, but we did it to make ourselves an example to you so that you would imitate us. In fact, when we were with you, this is what we commanded you: "If anyone isn't willing to work, he should not eat." For we hear that there are some among you who walk irresponsibly, not working at all, but interfering with the work of others. Now we command and exhort such people by the Lord Jesus Christ that quietly working, they may eat their own food. (2 Thess. 3:6-12)*

There is a lot here, so let's take this passage one step at a time. Just like Paul did 1 Thessalonians 4, he makes this a "command," but this time the command is different. This command is very serious. This is the only command, in all of Paul's writings, which is given "in the name of our Lord Jesus Christ." Could Paul have been any more serious when he made this command?

Paul "appeals" to them to pray fervently in Romans 15. Nine different times Paul "urges" people to display unity, to love, to live sacrificially for Christ, and to walk worthy of their calling, but here Paul "commands them in the name of our Lord Jesus Christ." The importance of what is coming next cannot be overstated. It could be argued that Paul believes this is the most important message he is going to deliver to the Thessalonians.

Paul introduces what is so important. They should "keep away from every brother who walks irresponsibly and not according to the tradition received from us." Paul actually instructs them to break the relationship, but what was the tradition of Paul? That he worked hard to provide for his own needs. Paul says those who don't do this are "irresponsible." Notice that Paul refers to those who do not work as "irresponsible" three times.

Paul reminds them that he and God's coworkers had a right to support, but they did not accept it because they did not want to be a "burden." If these believers worked so they weren't "a burden," then wouldn't the opposite be true? Those who are able to work, but don't, are a burden. Paul also worked hard to set an example for others to follow. If working to care for your own needs is an example worthy of following, then those who do not work live a pattern that should not be imitated. Paul believed so strongly in this teaching that if any of his coworkers did not support themselves, they did not eat.

Paul started this teaching and he ends this teaching with a command in the name of the "Lord Jesus Christ." How much more of a priority can he put on this instruction? There is not any other passage of Scripture that Paul wrote with this high of a priority. So what was the final command in this section? To work quietly and eat their own food.

Final words are important. They are the last thing heard and often the first thing people remember. Living out God's plan to work and independently provide for our own needs is the final instruction Paul gave to the Thessalonian church. Paul believed it, preached it, demanded it for his companions, and personally lived it out. Living out God's plan was a really big deal to Paul, but let's look at the ultimate example; Jesus.

One day I was having lunch with one of my pastors and he asked for my thoughts on how to help a homeless man who had come to the church and asked for assistance. The church had met his immediate need and offered to help with long-term solutions to his situation, but that was not the assistance the man wanted. He never came right out and blatantly asked for money, but he kept insinuating that he wanted the church to give him some. He was told we would not give him any money, but we were willing to help him get back on his feet so that he could begin to care for his own needs. That is when he pulled out the familiar line that many people like to use: "But what would Jesus do?"

That question got under my skin because a lot of people use that line. I often hear this question used to support the actions of blindly giving things to those in need. The truth is, we don't have a clue what Jesus would do. Jesus did not live in our time or in this type of society. I told my pastor, "I think we need to change that from WWJD to WDJD: What Did Jesus Do?" We can't be sure what Jesus would do in many situations, but we have written records of what Jesus did and didn't do. So what did Jesus do?

When Jesus showed up, everything was open to a new interpretation. He changed the understanding of the sacrificial system in Matthew 9 when He said, "I desire mercy, not sacrifice." He consistently told the religious leaders He wanted more than their rituals and traditions. He broke the accepted standards on the Sabbath, interacting with "unclean" people, and teaching women. He changed the rules on divorce and swearing oaths. He really mixed things up in Matthew 5 when he said the motivation of the heart was a higher standard than the letter of the law.

So if Jesus wanted to change God's plan, you would think it would be pretty obvious in the New Testament. Now, there are a lot of things that He specifically addressed that needed to be changed. Jesus clarified the rules to provide a better or deeper understanding of what it meant to follow Him. He set an entirely new standard for His people on so many different topics and with all the changes He made, He certainly had the opportunity to change the understanding of God's plan.

He could have turned the entire "work to provide for your own needs" plan on its head. But with all the changes Jesus brought, that one He didn't change. Jesus only provided deeper understanding on areas of life and the Law that had been misinterpreted or misapplied. If He remained silent on a subject and did not lead anyone to write a correction to it, we have to believe He did not want it changed. But did Jesus really remain silent on God's plan?

Just like in Genesis, there is not a passage where Jesus says, "I command people to work and care for themselves." Although, a lack of a direct reference doesn't mean He didn't have any thoughts on the subject. There are a lot of people who have the opinion that Jesus would give things to anyone in need. These people think, *we love people like Jesus did because we give clothes and food*, but there are no examples of this in Jesus' life. In fact, when you look at the life of Christ, I think you may be surprised when you see how Jesus' heart to care for the poor played out in His own ministry. Sadly, we have allowed our belief system to shape Scripture instead of Scripture shaping our belief system.

So what does the life of Jesus show us about His thoughts on God's plan? First, Scripture tells us the profession of Joseph (Jesus' earthly father). Why is this important enough to be recorded? There could be several reasons. It certainly shows that Jesus was a common man and not the royal prince they were looking for, but this also affirms the system in which Jesus was born. Joseph was a carpenter and in the tradition of the day, taught his son to be a carpenter as well.

That's right. Jesus had a job. He learned the trade of his earthly father. This fact is often overlooked because Scripture is silent on the vast majority of Jesus' life. All four gospels focus on His public ministry, but for nearly 90 percent of Jesus' earthly life Scripture is silent. He got up, went to work, ate, slept, and lived a "normal" life. We see His birth, one instance when He was twelve, and then His public ministry. Other than Mary, Joseph, and a few family members, there is no evidence to show that anyone even knew He was the son of God before the age of thirty. He was simply known as Joseph's son or the carpenter (Matt 13:55; Mark 6:3).

I can tell you from personal experience, carpentry is hard work. For several years I owned a remodeling company. It's exhausting: sore muscles, calloused hands, and the occasional smashed thumb. The life of a carpenter is not easy. I can't imagine how much harder Jesus had to work than I did, because He had to do it all without the use of air compressors, table saws, screw guns, and pickup trucks. Regardless of how hard it was, Jesus entered into the system and He Himself worked.

The people who Jesus chose to surround Himself with in ministry worked. Again, for some reason, Scripture documents the careers of some of His closest companions. The Bible lists the occupations of six of the twelve disciples. Peter, Andrew, James, and John were fisherman. Simon was a political activist and Matthew was a tax collector. There is no record of the careers of the other disciples, but it is believed by many theologians that

59

Judas was a banker because Jesus put him in charge of the money. Luke, who was not a disciple, but was very active in ministry and wrote the book that carries his name, was a doctor and as we saw earlier, Paul was a tentmaker.

Why is this important? Because it helps us understand each of them, and it shows that Jesus and His followers lived within the created system. He got rid of, changed, or brought a deeper understanding to the parts of life and the law that were misunderstood. But when it came to God's plan, He didn't abolish it. He didn't change it. He didn't bring a new understanding of it. He lived within it and even supported it.

Jesus' teachings acknowledged and reinforced God's plan for people to work to provide for their own needs. One of Jesus' teaching methods was to use parables. They were used to provide one of the Fundamental Elements to His followers, *instruction*, but His parables were based on real-life situations. So what can we learn about Jesus' thoughts on work through the parables?

Jesus included the fact that people worked in the vast majority of His parables. There is discrepancy on how many parables there are. Some say as few as thirty and others say more than sixty, but when looking at these parables, over 90 percent acknowledge that people worked. I know of no other topic that is covered over 90 percent of the time. I find that astounding.

In these parables, Jesus often praises those who work and never praises someone who doesn't. Let's look specifically at what Jesus says about work in the parable of the talents.

> *"For it is just like a man going on a journey. He called his own slaves and turned over his possessions to them. To one he gave five talents; to another, two; and to another, one—to each according to his own ability. Then he went on a journey. Immediately the man who had received five talents went, put them to work, and earned five more. In the same way the man*

with two earned two more. But the man who had received one talent went off, dug a hole in the ground, and hid his master's money. After a long time the master of those slaves came and settled accounts with them. The man who had received five talents approached, presented five more talents, and said, 'Master, you gave me five talents. Look, I've earned five more talents.' His master said to him, 'Well done, good and faithful slave! You were faithful over a few things; I will put you in charge of many things. Share your master's joy!' Then the man with two talents also approached. He said, 'Master, you gave me two talents. Look, I've earned two more talents.' His master said to him, 'Well done, good and faithful slave! You were faithful over a few things; I will put you in charge of many things. Share your master's joy!' Then the man who had received one talent also approached and said, 'Master, I know you. You're a difficult man, reaping where you haven't sown and gathering where you haven't scattered seed. So I was afraid and went off and hid your talent in the ground. Look, you have what is yours.' But his master replied to him, 'You evil, lazy slave! If you knew that I reap where I haven't sown and gather where I haven't scattered, then you should have deposited my money with the bankers. And when I returned I would have received my money back with interest. So take the talent from him and give it to the one who has 10 talents. For to everyone who has, more will be given, and he will have more than enough. But from the one who does not have, even what he has will be taken away from him. And throw this good-for-nothing slave into the outer darkness. In that place there will be weeping and gnashing of teeth.'" (Matt. 25:14-30)

There are two very different responses given to the slaves. The first man "put the money to work" and doubled the money. He was rewarded and earned the title of "good and faithful." The second man took his money and "in the same way" doubled the money. He was also rewarded and earned the title of "good and faithful." But the third man did not put the money to work, was punished, and earned different titles. His titles were "evil," "lazy," and "good for nothing." Other translations use the words *wicked, useless, slothful,* and *worthless.*

Let that sink in for a minute. These are words in red. These are the words of Jesus. Let's not overlook that fact. He was the one telling them the parable. He was the one praising those who worked, and He was the one who used the words *evil, lazy, good for nothing, wicked, useless, slothful,* and *worthless.* Have you ever thought about those being Jesus' words? It seems to me He was supporting God's plan.

Not only did the parables acknowledge and support God's plan, but the miracles Jesus performed did too. All thirty-seven of the recognized miracles of Jesus provide at least one of the first three Fundamental Elements. Let's look at a few examples. The twenty-four miracles where Jesus healed someone with a birth defect or debilitating disease gave them the resources or opportunity to work and provide for themselves. Once again, we have to put these miracles into the context of the times.

In New Testament times a birth defect or skin disease was viewed by society and religious leaders as a punishment for some kind of sin, either from the parents or the child. John 9 gives us the perfect example of this when Jesus is asked by His disciples who it was that caused the blindness, the man or his parents. People who were born with birth defects were viewed as sinful and unclean and were shut out from society. In this case, like the other cases of people who were blind, deaf, mute, or crippled, the man was a beggar because there were little to no opportunities for people with disabilities to engage in work.

According to the law, a person with leprosy was required to live outside of the camp or city alone, or only with other diseased people. He would have worn torn clothing to show others his skin disease and, if he was around people, he had to put his hand over his mouth and yell, "Unclean, unclean." These rules obviously kept these people from engaging in work or in relationships with the rest of society. Those who were demon possessed were also shut out from society, but when Jesus healed any of these conditions, people were able to reenter society as well as care for themselves and their families.

Many of the miracles provided Jesus the opportunity for instruction. People learned who Jesus was and wanted to learn more about Him. Jesus used the healing of the centurion's servant (Matt. 8) to give instruction, and when Jesus fed the four thousand and the five thousand, He removed the distraction of a growling stomach so the people could learn. When Jesus instructed Simon to catch the fish with a coin in its mouth to pay taxes and when He killed the fig tree that produced no fruit, both of these had an instructional purpose.

Here is the amazing part about the miracles of Jesus, which show that relationships are the most important element. Every single miracle of Jesus, that's all thirty-seven of them, provided a relational aspect. They all opened the door to a relationship with Him or relationships with others. I was meeting with a pastor one day going through this material and he said, "OK, what about the woman with the issue of blood?"

"Seriously, give me a hard one," I said. "In those days a woman with an issue of blood would have been required by Jewish law to sleep in a separate tent from her husband. She would have been unable to have any physical contact with him, her children, or anyone else. She was unclean—for twelve years—and that kept her isolated from society and her family."

Even the very first miracle of Jesus provided resources and relationships to be maintained. In the days of Jesus, it would have been considered a horrible offense to throw a wedding party and not have enough wine to serve your guests. When Jesus turned the water into wine, He not only saved the party, He allowed the family to be saved from public disgrace. Not providing properly could have cost them the ability to sell or barter and provide for their family. Jesus' miracles show God's plan by providing resources, opportunities, instructions, or relationships.

Jesus also put a very high priority on His own personal relationships. He had a lot of followers, but specifically chose twelve men to share life with as they learned from Him. Out of those twelve, He had three close companions who shared private moments. Out of the three, there was one, John, whom Jesus loved. Love is a relational word.

What are the attributes of healthy relationships? Honesty, integrity, trust, mutual respect, and enjoying time together, but all of this must be based in love. Love is the most powerful attribute of relationships. Love is the bedrock upon which relationships must be built. Not the superficial type of love we see broadcast into our homes each night, or the sappy love which is the basis of so many movies my wife asks me to watch. That type of love is not really love at all.

According to 1 Corinthians 13, if we display all forms of spiritual gifts, but we do not have love for others, we are nothing. If we spend our lives on behalf of others, give away all we have for the poor, and even offer ourselves up to be burned in the place of someone else, but these actions are not motivated by love, we gain nothing. Love must be the basis of our actions and relationships.

We read further to learn what love is and what love isn't. It is patient and kind. It doesn't want what others have, it doesn't brag, and it's not conceited. Love does not act improperly, it is not selfish, it isn't angry, and it doesn't hold grudges. Love finds joy in truth. It bears burdens, believes, hopes, and endures. Love never ends.

Chapter 13 goes on to say that the gifts of the Spirit, knowledge, languages, and all earthly wisdom will one day die. Paul makes it clear that everything will come to an end, but only three things will remain throughout eternity: faith, hope, and love. The chapter ends with the understanding that of these three eternal attributes, the greatest is the basis of relationships—love.

Jesus showed the importance of love in Matthew 22. The Pharisees heard that Jesus had silenced the Sadducees, and they came together to devise a plan to trap Jesus.

> And one of them, an expert in the law, asked a question to test Him: "Teacher, which commandment in the law is the greatest?" He said to him, "Love the Lord your God with all your heart, with all your soul, and with all your mind. This is the greatest and most important commandment. The second is like it: Love your neighbor as yourself. All the Law and the Prophets depend on these two commandments." (Matt. 22:35-40)

According to Jesus, everything that God said through the Torah (Old Testament Law) and through His prophets can be boiled down to one thing: *love.* Loving God and loving others. There is no higher standard. Love requires relationships and relationships are the key to every aspect of ministry. Jesus did not overturn God's plan for people to work to provide for their own needs. His own life, words, and ministry show us that He supported God's plan.

DISCUSSION QUESTIONS

1. What are your thoughts on Paul's command to "keep away" from people who are "irresponsible" and don't work?
2. Do we still see people who are able to work to provide for themselves, but don't as "irresponsible"?
3. Why would Paul put such a huge emphasis on this command to work?
4. How does the ministry of Jesus to the poor change your thoughts on serving "the least of these"?
5. What are some ways that Jesus "loved" the poor?
6. How does the statement "What Did Jesus Do?" change your thoughts on serving the poor?
7. What does the description of love in 1 Corinthians 13 reveal about those who don't work to care for themselves?

CHAPTER 5

GOD'S PLAN FOR THE POOR

A quick search of the Internet can result in some pretty sobering statistics. There are 925 million people in the world who suffer from a lack of nourishment.[1] The numbers vary, but somewhere between 29 and 30 thousand children under the age of five die every day from preventable diseases. That's roughly 11 million children per year.[2] There are at least 143 million orphans worldwide.[3] There are obviously a lot of poor and hurting people in the world.

Let's zoom in a little closer. According to the 2010 US Census, there are 48.5 million people living in poverty in the United States.[4] That's over 15 percent of the US population unable to meet their basic needs without assistance. Move in a little closer still and you'll find that 415,861 households in Tennessee are receiving food stamps[5] and 114,063 of my neighbors in Nashville are living in poverty.[6] The statistics paint a pretty bleak picture, but statistics don't feel pain.

What about the little girl on free and reduced lunch who doesn't get food when school is out? What about the boy in the inner city who wants attention, but his mom is working two jobs, there is no man around, and the gang is the only group that is there? What about the men and women sitting in our jails and prisons just waiting out their time? What about the homeless family we pass on our way to church? Those are real people, they do feel pain, and they are looking for real answers.

Now I understand that up to this point we have been focused solely on God's plan for people to be independent and care for their own needs, but there is another side to God's plan and it concerns our service to the poor. God loves the poor and hurting. They hold a very special place in His heart. Jesus spent a lot of time talking about caring for the poor. Jesus didn't suggest it. In Matthew 6 He said, "When you give to the poor" (notice the *when*). He made it perfectly clear that we are to care for the poor. It is expected—not optional—behavior for His followers.

In Matthew 25, Jesus tells His disciples what will happen on Judgment Day. Those who fed the hungry, gave a drink to the thirsty, took in the stranger, or visited the sick and those in prison are all rewarded with eternal life. Those who did not do these things are eternally punished. Jesus puts an exclamation point on this teaching by saying when you did these things for "the least of these brothers of mine, you did it for Me." Jesus clearly taught that we serve Him by serving the poor, but what does it mean to serve the poor?

Is there a right or wrong way to serve? Does it even matter if it is right or wrong? Aren't we commanded to serve? Isn't serving an act of obedience and that is what's important? Are we supposed to make a difference or just obey?

In Mark 14:7 Jesus said, "You will always have the poor with you." That's not a great outlook on life, so maybe the point is just to help them any way we can, but He goes on to say, "And you can do what is good for them whenever you want." So we are expected to "do what is good for them." I was happy to learn that there is a bigger purpose to serving than just obeying for the sake of obedience. So what is good for the poor? Does God have anything to say to us about how we are to care for them?

God consistently instructed His children to care for the poor, but He didn't leave them unprepared with a lot of questions that needed to be answered on how to serve. He set up an entire system of guidelines, in Leviticus and Deuteronomy, so they would be served and served properly. He expects His people to serve, but to serve in the correct way. God's plan includes instruction on how to serve the poor. Therefore, how we serve matters. We find some of God's instruction in Leviticus 19.

> *"When you reap the harvest of your land, you are not to reap to the very edge of your field or gather the gleanings of your harvest. You must not strip your vineyard bare or gather its fallen grapes. Leave them for the poor and the foreign resident; I am Yahweh your God."* (Lev. 19:9-10)

And again in Leviticus 23.

> *"When you reap the harvest of your land, you are not to reap all the way to the edge of your field or gather the gleanings of your harvest. Leave them for the poor and the foreign resident; I am Yahweh your God."* (Lev. 23:22)

God provided for the poor, but it doesn't look like any type of system I see represented in our society. God gave instructions to leave the food for the poor. They would get their food, but they had to come and get it for themselves. God did not say, *Reap all the way to the edges of your field and take a portion of it to the poor*. There was no instruction for them to, *reap all the way to the edges of your field and set up a food bank for the poor to come and get the food*. God provided for the poor, but they had to work for it. There is a continuation of this instruction in Deuteronomy.

> *"When you reap the harvest in your field, and you forget a sheaf in the field, do not go back to get it. It*

is to be left for the foreign resident, the fatherless, and the widow, so that the LORD your God may bless you in all the work of your hands. When you knock down the fruit from your olive tree, you must not go over the branches again. What remains will be for the foreign resident, the fatherless, and the widow. When you gather the grapes of your vineyard, you must not glean what is left. What remains will be for the foreign resident, the fatherless, and the widow."
(Deut. 24:19-21)

In the above verses God repeats Himself three times, which increases the importance of the instruction. When you gather the harvest and forget a sheaf in the field (a sheaf is a pile of product that has already been bundled up and is ready to be taken to the barn for storage), don't go back and pick it up. Instead, *leave it for the poor.* When you harvest your olive trees, don't go over the trees a second time. Instead, *leave it for the poor.* When harvesting your vineyards, don't go back and take a second pass. Instead, *leave it for the poor.*

God instructed the Israelites to care for the poor in a certain way. He provided the necessary food, but the poor had to come and do the work. This instruction comes with a promise. Why leave it for the poor? So that "God may bless you in all the work of your hands." Just to make this clear: By leaving it there for the poor, God would bless the farmer. He didn't say, *I will bless you if you go and get what you forgot and take it to the poor.*

Let's think back to God's plan. God's plan was for people to work to provide for their own needs, and God provided resources, opportunity, and instruction for those needs to be met. His desire for that to happen, as part of our service to the poor, is seen in this instruction to the Israelites. His plan is for the poor to work for their own food. God's plan has never included giveaway programs or handouts.

Today, many of the poor in our society are provided for without having to do anything. They ask for help and are given everything they need, but that is not what we see in Scripture. I am unaware of even one example where Jesus gave someone food or provided for them so they didn't have to work. In fact, other than the parable of the Good Samaritan, I can't even find an example where Jesus referenced giving extended support to someone who had fallen on hard times. And, in the story of the Good Samaritan, the help he received returned him to health so he could once again provide for himself. There are only a few examples, in both the Old and New Testaments, of God providing for people and each time it was a situational response and not the norm.

- God provided for the children of Israel in the dessert with manna and quail (Exodus 16)
- God miraculously provided flour and oil for a widow during a three-year drought while Elijah, the prophet, lived with her and her son (1 Kings 17)
- God multiplied oil for a widow so she could pay off her debt (2 Kings 4)

I can only find two examples of God providing food for an individual, and it was to meet a very specific need.

- God commanded the ravens to bring bread and meat to Elijah while he was in the wilderness (1 Kings 17)
- God had an angel make bread for Elijah while he was in the wilderness (1 Kings 19)

There are three times that God multiplied a small amount of food to feed larger groups.

- A hundred men were fed with twenty loaves of bread (2 Kings 4)
- Jesus fed five thousand men (not including women and children) with five loaves of bread and two fish (Mark 6)

- Jesus fed four thousand men (not including women and children) with seven loaves of bread and a few small fish (Mark 8)

There may be a few others I've missed, but I came up with eight times. Two times were long-term provision when there was no other option available, once was to help a widow who had no support, and five times food was provided to meet very specific needs. Let's put this in context. The Bible was written over a 1,400-year period and covers roughly four thousand years of history, and only eight times is it recorded that God gave people food that they did not work for. That's an average of once every five hundred years.

God's plan was not for the poor to be given everything they wanted and/or needed. God's desire was for the poor to get what they needed by working for it. God's plan for people to work for their own provision wasn't for the wealthy or middle class alone. His plan included the poor. He wanted the poor to care for themselves. When the children of Israel followed God's plan, the poor received everything they needed.

God's plan provided ways for the poor to gather their own food and meet their own needs. God even made sure food was available for them during times when no harvest would be gathered. God called His people to give the land a Sabbath rest. Just like they were to rest every seventh day, the land was to rest every seventh year, but God didn't leave the poor out. God made provisions for the poor during the Sabbath year.

> *"Sow your land for six years and gather its produce. But during the seventh year you are to let it rest and leave it uncultivated, so that the poor among your people may eat from it and the wild animals may consume what they leave. Do the same with your vineyard and your olive grove."* (Exod. 23:10-11)

During the Sabbath year, the poor were still given the opportunity to care for themselves. We also see this instruction given a second time in Leviticus.

> The LORD spoke to Moses on Mount Sinai: "Speak to the Israelites and tell them: When you enter the land I am giving you, the land will observe a Sabbath to the LORD. You may sow your field for six years, and you may prune your vineyard and gather its produce for six years. But there will be a Sabbath of complete rest for the land in the seventh year, a Sabbath to the LORD: you are not to sow your field or prune your vineyard. You are not to reap what grows by itself from your crop, or harvest the grapes of your untended vines. It must be a year of complete rest for the land. Whatever the land produces during the Sabbath year can be food for you—for yourself, your male or female slave, and the hired hand or foreigner who stays with you. All of its growth may serve as food for your livestock and the wild animals in your land." (Lev. 25:1-7)

This provision is a good start, but God's plan gets even better. He went a step further to provide hope. God gave hope for the poor that, one day, they would be able to break free from the circumstances holding them down. God gave opportunities for the poor to be restored. It is God's desire for the poor to get back on their feet and live life to its fullest. They didn't have to remain servants and they didn't have to remain poor. Look at the additional instructions God gave concerning the Sabbath year.

Deuteronomy 15 begins with the instruction that the children of Israel are to cancel debts at the end of every seven years. Over the next few verses God gives very specific instructions about how the debts are to be cancelled. God even warns them not to be hardhearted or tightfisted towards the poor in the years leading up to the time when the debt would be forgiven. The instruction was to lend them whatever they needed, even if there was only a year or two before the Sabbath year. Then God says this:

> "Give to him, and don't have a stingy heart when you give, and because of this the LORD your God will bless you in all your work and in everything you do. For there will never cease to be poor people in the land; that is why I am commanding you, 'You must willingly open your hand to your afflicted and poor brother in your land.' If your fellow Hebrew, a man or woman, is sold to you and serves you six years, you must set him free in the seventh year. When you set him free, do not send him away empty-handed. Give generously to him from your flock, your threshing floor, and your winepress. You are to give him whatever the LORD your God has blessed you with."
> (Deut. 15:10-14)

Every seven years the Hebrews were freed from debt, but they were also free from servitude. They did not have to continue to work for someone else. They could return to their family land with a fresh start, but if they were poor, they wouldn't have the needed supplies to start over and grow their own crops. God took care of that by telling their masters, "Give him whatever the LORD your God has blessed you with." Through these gifts, God was giving the poor the chance at a new beginning.

This is the pinnacle of Sabbath law. Do not hold back from the poor who are going to be returning to their own land. In the RKV (Rob Kendall Version) it reads something like this.

> Give graciously and the Lord your God will bless you. You will always have the poor among you, but that's

why I am telling you to care for them, and how do I want you to do this? When you set your brother free, don't send him away with nothing. Give generously to him of everything that God has blessed you with. Give him male and female animals so that he can go and breed his own cattle. Give him seeds so that he will be able to grow produce in his own fields and vineyards. Give him something to eat and drink so he doesn't die along the road on the trip home.

This command is God's way of opening the door to provide the two elements they were lacking. They had the instruction because they had been working for someone else for the last few years. They had some of the resources at their disposal because they were Hebrews and had an inheritance in the land which they were returning to, but they were missing the resources necessary to start over. Here, they were given the opportunity and the missing resources to rebuild their families. This command provides both of the missing Fundamental Elements: Resources and Opportunity. It also mirrors the promise found in Deuteronomy 24 that if they obey this command, things will go well with them.

God gave the Hebrews a chance to start over every seven years, but what about foreigners in the land? Were they left hopeless without any chance of being set free? No, God ordered a Year of Jubilee when *all* the residents of the land were to be set free.

"You are to count seven sabbatical years, seven times seven years, so that the time period of the seven sabbatical years amounts to 49. Then you are to sound a trumpet loudly in the seventh month, on the tenth day of the month; you will sound it throughout your land on the Day of Atonement. You are to

consecrate the fiftieth year and proclaim freedom in the land for all its inhabitants. It will be your Jubilee, when each of you is to return to his property and each of you to his clan. The fiftieth year will be your Jubilee; you are not to sow, reap what grows by itself, or harvest its untended vines. It is to be holy to you because it is the Jubilee; you may only eat its produce directly from the field. In this Year of Jubilee, each of you will return to his property." (Lev. 25:8-13)

After the seventh sabbatical there was to be an additional year of rest, but God called for more than just a second year of rest. This section tells us that everyone was instructed to go back to their family land because it was their Jubilee. The Year of Jubilee was a chance for people to be reunited with their families. This was their chance to start over. They no longer had to be servants—they were given the opportunity to go home and rebuild their families.

The passage goes on, for the remainder of chapter 25, about the Year of Jubilee. We learn the rules for buying and selling land. We learn how it can be purchased back before the Year of Jubilee. We see special rules for the Levites. We also see that all property which had been sold is to be returned to the owner during the Year of Jubilee.

There is only one exception to this rule. A home that is built within a walled city would not be returned during the Year of Jubilee. This exception interested me. Why would God call for this exception? What is it about a home in a walled city that would make it different?

God starts His explanation by reminding His people that they were considered foreigners and temporary residents on His property. God didn't want them to get overconfident and think they were the ones in charge. They needed to remember that He is the one who directs their paths. He is their God, but there is more to it than that. If this was done as only a reminder that He owned everything, why didn't He keep the same rules for land and houses owned in cities that are not walled?

Because God did not want to stop their ability to care for themselves. A home in a walled city would have been a convenience for trade and business, but would not have been a necessity. There would be no crops grown on that property and the property would not produce any income. The fields to grow their crops, graze their cattle, and provide for their families were located in the country, or in cities without walls. God made a way for them to meet their needs, but He didn't guarantee their wants. God protected a person's ability to work, but did not protect the niceties of life.

As I continued to study and reflect on all the opportunities God provided for the poor, I realized we currently face a tragedy that would not have existed in Old Testament times when they used God's plan to serve the poor. In His plan, the Year of Jubilee gave the poor a chance at a do-over. Every fifty years, struggling families were given a mulligan (a golf term for when a golfer gets the opportunity to do a shot over). A generation is twenty-five to thirty years, so no family would have been forced to continue in poverty beyond the fifty-year mark. When the children of Israel followed God's plan, there would be no generational poverty.

The idea that the poor should be required to perform some type of work to gain the necessities of life flies in the face of many of the thoughts, programs, and services offered today. Often the "assistance" our government programs gives to the poor actually punishes people for trying to work and take care of themselves. Meredith and I have seen this reality many times in the lives of the men and women we serve. They get a job and gain an income, but the cuts in each of the numerous programs they have grown to rely on outweigh the income they receive. It's easier for them to quit their jobs, get their benefits reinstated, and stay on government assistance. They can always go to churches and nonprofits for additional help.

The subtitle of this book is "Debunking the Myth of Social Justice." There are certain aspects of social justice that are good, but there are many that are not. The good part of social justice is found in the dignity of every human being. We are all created equal. Those who preach social justice believe we all have the right to gain the resources, opportunity, and instruction necessary to meet our basic needs, but these are not new teachings. They are straight out of Scripture and are laid as the groundwork for social justice. Unfortunately, as the theory of social justice has evolved, it has begun to go against God's plan for humanity.

Today, social justice focuses more on giving and distributing than it does on gaining and creating. It seeks to provide preferential treatment for certain groups by forcing a "just" outcome, but who gets to decide what's "just"? Social justice creates top-heavy systems run by distant, detached people who are more concerned with rules and regulations than what is best for those being served. Social justice is reduced to a transaction. The benefits of social justice are a myth and do not exist.

Now this may, once again, appear to have taken a political turn, but trust me, this isn't political. It's biblical. As I said earlier, I don't trust the government to have any answers for the poor. I look to God for real answers. God created things to work a certain way, and I am opposed to anything that goes against His plan and systems.

God says we should not deny justice to the poor, but we are also not to give preferential treatment to the poor, which often is the goal of social justice.

> "You must not spread a false report. Do not join the
> wicked to be a malicious witness. You must not
> follow a crowd in wrongdoing. Do not testify in a

lawsuit and go along with a crowd to pervert justice.
Do not show favoritism to a poor person in his
lawsuit. If you come across your enemy's stray ox
or donkey, you must return it to him. If you see
the donkey of someone who hates you lying helpless
under its load, and you want to refrain from helping
it, you must help with it. You must not deny justice
to a poor person among you in his lawsuit."
(Exod. 23:1-6)

God calls for justice for everyone, but God wants more than social justice. God's plan provides *restorative* justice. Restorative justice is always better than social justice. God's plan provides what is best for every person involved: those who are rich and comfortable, and those who are poor and hurting.

God's call for the poor to care for themselves and meet their own needs is taught in the New Testament also. God set up guidelines and boundaries just like He did in the Old Testament. We've already seen Paul's examples and teachings. We've seen God's plan in the life and ministry of Jesus, but Paul gives additional instruction. It is covered in the book of Timothy and specifically concerns care for widows.

Support widows who are genuinely widows. But if
any widow has children or grandchildren, they must
learn to practice godliness toward their own family
first and to repay their parents, for this pleases God.
The real widow, left all alone, has put her hope in God
and continues night and day in her petitions and
prayers; however, she who is self-indulgent is dead
even while she lives. Command this also, so they
won't be blamed. But if anyone does not provide for
his own, that is his own household, he has denied the
faith and is worse than an unbeliever. No widow

should be placed on the official support list unless she is at least 60 years old, has been the wife of one husband, and is well known for good works—that is, if she has brought up children, shown hospitality, washed the saints' feet, helped the afflicted, and devoted herself to every good work. But refuse to enroll younger widows, for when they are drawn away from Christ by desire, they want to marry and will therefore receive condemnation because they have renounced their original pledge. At the same time, they also learn to be idle, going from house to house; they are not only idle, but are also gossips and busybodies, saying things they shouldn't say. Therefore, I want younger women to marry, have children, manage their households, and give the adversary no opportunity to accuse us. For some have already turned away to follow Satan. If any believing woman has widows in her family, she should help them, and the church should not be burdened, so that it can help those who are genuinely widows. (1 Tim. 5:3-16)

Paul lays out some pretty tough teaching here concerning the care provided to widows. To put someone on the "official support list" of the church meant to care for their financial needs, but in turn they would work within the body. They still had to work. If they were young, they should not be put on the list at all. They should take responsibility for their lives and families, and care for their own needs.

Did you notice what was written in verse 8? *"But if anyone does not provide for his own, that is his own household, he has denied the faith and is worse than an unbeliever."* We see once again that Paul believes working to care for our families is an attribute of those who follow Christ. Not doing so means that you have "denied the faith."

The last point from this passage is the call for family members to care for their own and not have them be a burden on the church. Helping people who are able to help themselves takes vital resources that could be used for others who are truly in need. This hurts those served and those serving and creates frustration, distrust, and antagonism. God calls us to help the poor, but we are to help in the proper way. God's plan provides what is best for everyone involved. The antagonism and frustration that drives wedges between us can be eliminated. Now we need to learn the difference between those who are truly in need and those who should be caring for themselves.

DISCUSSION QUESTIONS

1. What patterns do you see in God's care for the poor?
2. For what reason have we established so many feeding programs when God did not give us this example from His care for the poor?
3. How would our society change if we still honored the Sabbatical laws?
4. What would be some positive and negative results if we properly equipped inner-city communities and then made them responsible for the results?
5. What is the difference between providing *social* justice and providing *restorative* justice?
6. Can you think of some examples of the antagonism that has grown between those serving and those served?

CHAPTER 6

THE CAN'TS, DON'TS, AND WON'TS

W e tend to be a black-and-white, all-or-nothing society. This reality has caused most of us to either adopt passages of Scripture calling for people to work and provide their own needs or passages calling us to care for others. I can appreciate these one-sided responses. On the surface it would appear that Scripture contradicts itself. One calls for people to be independent and the other calls us to serve. As we learned in the last chapter, God's plan and those opposing verses seamlessly work together. Unfortunately, this apparent contradiction has caused confusion about serving those in need and has resulted in two distinct approaches that come from two diametrically opposed viewpoints.

The first response is based on verses instructing us to work hard. Those of us in this camp believe people should get jobs and "pull themselves up by their bootstraps." We close our hearts and wallets. We tend to categorize, stereotype, and label the poor as a drain on society. *They are lazy and need to get a job and take care of themselves.* We have given up on helping.

The second response is based on verses instructing us to serve the poor. Those of us in this camp believe people would get jobs if they could, but they are the unfortunate, weak, and suffering—they need to be taken care of. We open our hearts and wallets and provide all the "necessities." We tend to categorize, stereotype, and label the poor as hopeless victims. *They need to be fed, housed, and provided for.* We willingly give and serve anyone in need.

Both of these responses are obviously taken to the extreme, but they are the basis of the two opposing viewpoints. As we learned in the last chapter, neither of them represent God. One says to disengage and the other says to improperly engage. Self-care and caring for the poor don't seem to mesh well. So how do we find unity from these two opposing viewpoints?

First, we have to understand how we got to where we are. The poor were not part of God's original creation. They did not and would not have existed if sin had not entered the world. Suffering and poverty are the results of sin. That statement is not a slap at people who are hurting or a claim that they are being punished because of their sin. The truth is, there are people who have value and are created in the image of God who need assistance because we live in a fallen world.

Sin corrupted God's creation and God's plan. Sin impacted our ability to provide for ourselves and our ability to be in relationship with others. If sin had not entered the world, there would be no hungry children, no homelessness, and no poverty. If Adam and Eve had not eaten the fruit and disobeyed God, there would be no broken and hurting people. Suffering and poverty are the results of sin.

Sin has affected the motives and behaviors of everyone involved. Sin whispers in our ear that we should take care of our own needs and not worry about the needs of others. Sin tells us to operate from selfish motives. Sin's impact has affected both parties involved, those served *and* those serving. Some serve to gain their own personal accolades. Some receive to get from others what they should gain for themselves. So how do we serve in ways that are healthy for everyone involved?

The answer is found in a unified commitment to follow God's plan. Those who request assistance and those who are called to serve cannot interact in productive ways if there is not unity. When individuals, churches, and organizations operate from different sets of priorities, they confuse and hurt those they are called to serve. Our response must be consistent regardless of where someone goes for help. Disunity among those who serve is making the problem worse for everyone. It has driven wedges between those serving and those being served as people operate out of their own personal priorities and not a biblical standard.

So how do we represent God's plan today? The key is found in understanding why people need assistance. Everyone who carries the title of "poor" is not the same and in God's plan the reason someone becomes poor was a significant factor, and it makes a difference on how God calls us to respond. The reason there is confusion on how to help those in need is because we don't respond to each person based upon their situation.

Our approach to serving must meet the distinct needs of each individual person. A one-size-fits-all approach does not work well and adds to the problem. Neither side will receive what God has determined is best for them. Much of the poverty and many who are suffering are there because God's people have not followed His plan. God's plan provides guidelines, processes, and structure to our response.

There are many different people who knock on the doors of society asking for assistance. Many seek help out of actual need and some seek assistance from selfish motives. They may be men or women, single or married, parents or children. They may be in our own neighborhoods or on the other side of the world. They come in every shape, color, and size.

They all have their differences. They all operate from different intentions. They all have different stories, but as different as all of them are, they all can be classified into one of three groups. The Can'ts, the Don'ts, and the Won'ts. Let's get to know these people.

The Can'ts are easy to understand. The Can'ts *"cannot"* successfully gain the first three Fundamental Elements of God's plan for independence. They are physically or mentally incapable of caring for themselves. Many would like me to add emotionally incapable to that list, but we have to be very careful. This addition could easily be abused, by both those served and those serving, but I think we can leave some room for unique situations.

The Don'ts are the second group. The Don'ts *"do not"* have at least one of the first three Fundamental Elements in God's plan for independence. They are physically and mentally able to care for themselves, but are lacking resources, opportunities, or instructions. The Don'ts represent a large number of people who walk into our churches and nonprofits asking for assistance. The Don'ts are harder to recognize, but God never said serving Him would be easy.

The Won'ts are the third group. The Won'ts *"will not"* do the work. They are physically and mentally able to care for themselves, they have access to resources, opportunities, and instructions, but for whatever reason they choose not to work. Now I understand in our economy today that people have a hard time finding work. That's not what I'm talking about. At the same time, there are many others who use the economy as an excuse to sit back and do nothing.

Let's dig a little deeper into these groups because God's plan is unique for each of them. We need to understand the "why" of their struggle to respond appropriately. Responding to a request without understanding the "why" is not part of God's plan. Even within each category, a standardized response does not work well. Each person is unique and therefore each response must be adapted to their specific needs.

The Can'ts

There are several references to the Can'ts in the New Testament. Let's look at two. The first is found in Luke 7 (also recorded in Matthew 11) and the second is found in Matthew 15. In Luke, John the Baptist is about to be beheaded and he sends some of his disciples to make sure that Jesus is the real deal. I mean let's be honest, nobody wants to die for a false Messiah. John's disciples ask, "Are you the One, who is to come, or should we look for someone else?" I love how Jesus responds. He doesn't just answer the question with a yes or no, but shows that He is the fulfillment of the Old Testament prophecies concerning the Messiah. He tells John's disciples to go back and give John the following report.

> *He replied to them, "Go and report to John the things you have seen and heard: The blind receive their sight, the lame walk, those with skin diseases are healed, the deaf hear, the dead are raised, and the poor are told the good news." (Luke 7:22)*

In the Matthew 15 passage, Jesus has just come from healing a woman's daughter and He is about to feed the four thousand, who have been following Him for three days with no food.

> *Moving on from there, Jesus passed along the Sea of Galilee. He went up on a mountain and sat there, and large crowds came to Him, having with them the lame, the blind, the deformed, those unable to speak, and many others. They put them at His feet, and He healed them. So the crowd was amazed when they saw those unable to speak talking, the deformed restored, the lame walking, and the blind seeing. And they gave glory to the God of Israel. (Matt. 15:29-31)*

Those are the Can'ts: the lame, the blind, the crippled, the leper, the deaf, and the mute. I am sure we can think of others that would fit into this category, like the elderly and children, but those are the main ones. They are the ones who would have been shut out. Most of them would have been physically unable to provide for their families. Their days consisted of sitting by the entrance of the temple or on a main street begging for support. They would have gotten some relief from the church, but they would not have been able to become self-sufficient.

Although the Can'ts of biblical times are not the same as the Can'ts of today. When someone has a physical handicap, there are things that can be done to increase their abilities to engage in society and provide for their own needs. They may need additional support or special equipment, but it can be done. It is amazing to think about the medical and technological advances we have today that didn't exist even fifty years ago. The "chains that bind" many in our society have been or are being removed.

Let me give you an example. When I was a kid, I remember a gentleman at our church who would have been one of the Can'ts in biblical times. He was an amazing man with a good sense of humor, but his life wasn't easy. Like everyone else, he had a few things he had to overcome, but his challenges were unique. His biggest obstacle happened early into his adult life when he lost his sight, but he didn't let a lack of sight define his future. He went back to school, graduated, and began working for a company that helped blind people gain independence, but he needed help. So on a regular schedule, someone went to his office to read his mail to him, wrote his responses, and drove him to appointments. My dad was one of those people.

This gentleman is a perfect example to show that a physical challenge, which would have prohibited someone from being independent in biblical times, is something that can be overcome today. His challenge was one that could be overcome with some support. It was not easy. It took a lot of commitment from several people, but it was possible. Now, move forward forty years with the advancements of today. There are fewer physical challenges that completely exclude someone from becoming self-sufficient.

My wife's stepdad has Parkinson's disease. He is a very strong man with an extensive background in business from restaurant ownership to building and remodeling houses. He has always worked hard and provided for himself and his family, but those days are gone. He can no longer physically work, but he is not helpless. He told me that one of his biggest frustrations is people who "think they are being nice" when they try to do everything for him. It makes him feel like a charity case. His direct quote is, "Let me do it...I'm not useless!"

When we go visit Meredith's side of the family, he and I have an arrangement. Since he can no longer do most of the work around the house, I willingly help him with anything he asks me to do. I have installed handrails, repaired washing machines, and ripped up carpet. When we go to the hardware store to pick up materials I ask, "Do you want me to pull up to the door and get you the riding cart or do you want to walk into the store?" It is his decision. While we are actually doing the work, he's in charge and I only do what he says he can't handle. Even though I do 90 percent of the work, he is still the one calling the shots and he is the one repairing his home. I am just his helper.

We have a responsibility to care for those who can't care for themselves, but our service must provide dignity to those we serve. If I did the work by myself and did not include him in the repairs, it would be easier and take much less time, but my service would add to his struggle. We must serve the Can'ts while following God's example in the Old Testament. We must only do for them what they cannot do for themselves. We must be equally concerned with their emotional and mental needs as we are with their physical needs.

The Don'ts

The Don'ts require a different approach. We must not treat them as Can'ts. Scripture talks about the Don'ts and establishes a system for how they should be served. God's plan provided them with resources, opportunities, and instructions so they could care for themselves. We learned a lot about God's plan for the Don'ts in the previous chapter.

Rules were established that provided them with all they needed to live. They had at their disposal produce from both the fields and the vineyards. They had opportunities to gain seed and regular chances to return to their ancestral land. There was even the possibility of gaining cattle and sheep. God left little to question as to caring for the Dont's. The Dont's could gain everything they needed, but the Dont's faced unique challenges that needed to be addressed.

> "Do not oppress a hired hand who is poor and needy, whether one of your brothers or one of the foreigners residing within a town in your land. You are to pay him his wages each day before the sun sets, because he is poor and depends on them. Otherwise he will cry out to the LORD against you, and you will be held guilty." (Deut. 24:14-15)

God required His people to take special consideration to assist with the specific challenges that were faced by the Don'ts. They were instructed to pay them their wages every single day. This allowed the Don'ts to provide food for their families. They also would have the money needed to find somewhere to sleep. God gives them this warning, if you don't pay him and he complains, I will hold the offender guilty. There aren't too many other places in Scripture where God gives this type of warning.

> "When you make a loan of any kind to your neighbor, do not enter his house to collect what he offers as

security. You must stand outside while the man you are making the loan to brings the security out to you. If he is a poor man, you must not sleep in the garment he has given as security. Be sure to return it to him at sunset. Then he will sleep in it and bless you, and this will be counted as righteousness to you before the LORD your God." (Deut. 24:10-13)

These verses are the introduction to the two verses we looked at above. Don't keep a poor man's garment because that is all he has to sleep in. Again, God's blessing and/or curse is based upon the poor man's response to how he was assisted. If the poor bless us for the way they are treated, then God will bless us. If the poor curse us for the way they are treated, God will hold us responsible.

The most significant part of this section is found in verse 11. Don't invade this man's home looking for your collateral. Let's think about that for just a second. That is the first point God makes in this section. Why is this so important that God would put it as the first instruction in this section on caring for the Don'ts?

Imagine with me, a family in Old Testament times. They are sitting around the table, eating dinner and preparing to watch the latest Babylonian crime show on TV, when suddenly there is a knock at the door. Dad opens the door and a man comes barging into the house. "Y'all owe me money an' I need yer coat as collateral," he yells in a Southern accent. This is not the way God wants us to treat the poor, or anyone else for that matter.

How would you feel if someone walked into your home, in front of your spouse and children, and demanded your coat as security for a loan? It would be humiliating. You would instantly lose the respect of your loved ones and you would be disgraced. God never calls us to devalue people and humiliate them, although we might view going into debt a little differently if this scenario were possible.

The Don'ts are the working poor. They are also "the widow, the orphan, and the foreign resident in your land." They are completely capable of caring for themselves, but have unique situations that increase their struggle. God expects them to provide for their own needs, but He instructs us to give them dignity and value as we help them gain avenues to meet those needs. We must help them gain independence.

When someone new comes to Against the Grain, we spend some time getting to know them. We hear their stories and help them identify the patterns in their lives that are at the root of their struggles. We listen to their dreams. We identify their needs and help them come up with a plan to achieve those dreams. After developing their plan, we work together to help them gain the resources, opportunities, and instructions that are missing.

It may be an education. It may be a car. It may start with a minimum-wage job to help them build solid work habits and a positive employment history. Whatever it is, we help them gain it for themselves. We don't give it to them. They have to work for it. They have to take ownership of their own future. This puts them in charge of their life—they are not looked on as charity cases.

One of the greatest feelings I have experienced in the last thirteen years of ministry comes by watching someone overcome an obstacle that was holding them back. We helped them along the way and kept them focused on their goals, but *they* were the one doing the work.

Without trying to sound condescending, working with the Dont's is a lot like parenting. In fact, I have a lot of young ladies who look at me as a father figure. I also have a lot of children who call me Granddaddy Rob. There are few things as fun as walking through the mall and seeing the looks on the faces of the passersby when a group of young African American children come running up to Meredith and me, giving us hugs and calling us Granddaddy Rob and Grandma Meredith. It's heartwarming and amusing.

Our goal as parents is to raise our children to take care of themselves. Most parents work very hard to achieve this goal. While in our home, we help them identify their strengths and weaknesses and help them gain the elements they need to move out and care for themselves. We may help them overcome specific struggles when they're on their own, but only if it doesn't interfere with the parties we're having because they're finally gone. The point is, we want our children to become self-sufficient.

This is the same approach we began to use when we started AtG. In fact, Meredith's comment that started this entire process with the first young lady was, "I'll be your mom." We helped her overcome her specific challenges and helped her gain the elements she was missing. It wasn't easy, it wasn't fast, and it wasn't always fun. There were many times when she wanted to quit and she "ran away" for a few months, but she came back and we continued to work with her.

We treated her like family. This is the same approach we have used with every other person who has come and asked for assistance from AtG. We are willing to invest in them as much as they are willing to invest in themselves. Unfortunately, many of the people who call us don't want to break out of their negative cycles. They just want immediate help. They want a bill paid or money. That brings us to the last group.

The Won'ts

The Won'ts may be the hardest group to identify because they often will be dishonest about their situation. We have had people look us straight in the eyes and tell us bald-faced lies to get what they wanted. I know this is not a shock to many of you, but I wasn't ready for it when we started AtG. After a lot of trial and error, and being burned a few times, we have learned how to spot the Wont's a little quicker. Here are five things that we have learned to help us distinguish the Wont's from the Dont's.

1. They usually have incredible stories of personal struggle.
2. They are almost always the victim of some type of injustice that has been perpetrated against them.
3. Their need is an emergency that does not allow time to think through and investigate their situation.
4. They often get angry when you begin to ask questions about their story and may lead to accusations that you hate the poor.
5. They are not willing to make any personal investment to receive help.

The truth is, the Wont's have chosen to live off the generosity of others and not engage as productive members of society. They have everything they need to take care of themselves and become self-sufficient—they just won't do it. Paul talks extensively about the Won'ts. In chapter 4 we looked at Paul's teachings in 2 Thessalonians 3 as we learned about God's plan in the New Testament, but I would like to revisit this passage and look at it from a different angle. We saw Paul's thoughts on work, but I want us to see how he viewed the Won'ts. More importantly, I want us to see how he commands us to respond.

As we saw, Paul is talking about those who were "not working at all." Those are the Won'ts. Paul refers to the Won'ts as "irresponsible" three times in 2 Thessalonians 3. Paul tells the Thessalonians to "keep away" from these brothers. And just so there is not confusion on the matter, Paul tells them to break relationships with the Wont's two different times in this passage.

Now we command you, brothers, in the name of our Lord Jesus Christ, to keep away from every brother who walks irresponsibly and not according to the tradition received from us. (2 Thess. 3:6)

There are many passages that talk about the dangers of being idle. Here, Paul continues, stating their "irresponsible" behavior leads them to create trouble for others.

For we hear that there are some among you who walk irresponsibly, not working at all, but interfering with the work of others. (v. 11)

They disturb the unity within the body of Christ and the community at large. These brothers are intentionally looking to cause problems. They remind me of the third servant in the Matthew 25 passage who buried the master's talents. He was wicked, lazy, and good for nothing. The Won'ts are a drain on the resources of society. Paul felt so strongly about this that he begins this section with the separation from the Won'ts and states it again in verse 14:

And if anyone does not obey our instruction in this letter, take note of that person; don't associate with him, so that he may be ashamed.

Paul ends the segment in 2 Thessalonians 3 with these words:

Yet don't treat him as an enemy, but warn him as a brother. (v. 15)

This last verse is where we clearly see God's plan coming into play. It is where we see relationships enter into the equation of helping the Won'ts. We are to love them and not hate them. We are to love them like family or a close friend. The idea is to restore this person to their rightful place. This has to be done through relationships. Caring for ourselves, and helping them do the same, is one of the ways in which we show love to others.

Paul talks about this in 1 Thessalonians 4. In fact, he says it is an example of brotherly love to care for your own needs and not be a burden on anyone. Paul is teaching us that love should be displayed on both sides of the equation. Those who serve must love those who are served by serving in the proper way. Those who are served also need to display love by working to care for themselves. Is their expectation to use the resources of others a loving act? No, it is a selfish act that is unacceptable in God's plan.

> *About brotherly love: You don't need me to write you because you yourselves are taught by God to love one another. In fact, you are doing this toward all the brothers in the entire region of Macedonia. But we encourage you, brothers, to do so even more, to seek to lead a quiet life, to mind your own business, and to work with your own hands, as we commanded you, so that you may walk properly in the presence of outsiders and not be dependent on anyone.* (1 Thess. 4:9-12)

Against the Grain was started out of a desire to help one single mother get on her feet. As it grew and we worked with more women, we told them we would give them direction and help them gain the resources, opportunities, and instructions they needed through relationships, but we were not going to pay their bills and we were not going to do the hard work for them. Many of these women had been longtime recipients of thousands of dollars in social welfare programs, but their lives were not changing and they were teaching their children to repeat the same negative patterns. The women knew they were heading into uncharted territory and it wouldn't be easy. Our model of serving these women was influenced heavily by Paul's instruction in 1 Thessalonians, 2 Thessalonians, and his teaching on ways to properly serve widows in 1 Timothy 5.

We've used God's plan for over thirteen years with incredible results. We've seen lives changed. We've seen families begin to build new legacies. We have helped people gain an education, employment, and housing. God's plan provides restoration, but as

I moved through the sabbatical, I had to ask myself, what is so important about work? Why did God make work such an integral part of His plan?

DISCUSSION QUESTIONS

1. What has been your response to those in poverty up to this point? Do you tend to be a "give everything" or "give nothing" kind of person?
2. What are your thoughts on the fact that suffering and poverty are a result of sin?
3. How does the understanding that everyone who is suffering is not the same affect your view on serving the poor?
4. Why is understanding the "reason for poverty" important as we try to serve?
5. Have you ever considered the potential humiliation and frustration felt by those who want to care for themselves, but people keep doing things for them?
6. Why is "caring for yourself" a display of love to others?

CHAPTER 7

WHY WORK?

Work. The ultimate four-letter word. The thing that many of us try to get out of on a daily basis. Work is hard. Work takes effort. Work distracts us from the more important things in life. You know, the things we do when we're not working.

We spend more than a third of our weekdays working. In comparison, according to the National Sleep Foundation, the average adult spends only 6.9 hours a night sleeping.[1] While most of us define "work" as what we get paid to do, we don't get paid for all of our work. There are a lot of things we need or want to do that require work. Add the amount of time we spend getting our "honey-do" list done. By the time you "make Mama happy" and do whatever additional things that must be done, I would be willing to bet that most of us spend well over half our time working, traveling to and from work, or thinking about work to meet our needs.

If you're anything like I am, you have a love-hate relationship with God's plan for us to care for ourselves. I think most of us do. We want to work and then wish we didn't have to. I've never been a fan, but have always wanted to do it. We go to work so we can meet our needs and then spend the money gained from our labor enjoying life, which means we have to go back to work to make more money. It's a vicious cycle.

I was taught the importance of working to care for my own needs in my childhood. It was necessary for everyone to pitch in and do their part in the Kendall household. I am the youngest of seven children, and we all had to work for the house to operate properly. My mom and dad did not believe in paying us to clean up after ourselves. My parents still have a sign in their bathroom that says: *This is a self-cleaning bathroom...You make a mess...you clean it up!* Additional chores were just part of the deal. If you gained the reward of living in the house, you also gained the responsibility of taking care of it.

As I got older, I began doing some odd jobs for people in the neighborhood. I washed cars, raked leaves, and mowed lawns. I was always driven to make money, and if there was money to be made, I was usually willing to do the work. I think I was in junior high when I set my first goal concerning money. I wanted to be a millionaire by the time I was thirty. While this goal was based in pride, materialism, and comfort, I was willing to do the work to gain the million.

As my oldest brother and four sisters grew up and moved out, Rick and I were the only two left at home. We actually convinced my parents we should get an allowance. They granted the allowance, but we had to earn it. It didn't come cheap. It included additional chores that were things my mom and dad had been doing. In the Kendall household, money was never just given to us. If you wanted something, you had to work for it.

After the allowance was given, I was more than happy to work for a few weeks, but then the excitement faded away and I didn't want to do it anymore. One week I decided to skip my additional duties to see what would happen. After several attempts to get me to do them, my parents offered the work and, more importantly, my allowance to my brother. Rick did the work and

Rick got the pay, but I gained a lesson worth much more than the twenty-five cents I would have gotten for the week. That lesson has stuck with me for the rest of my life. I learned you have to work for what you want.

I got my first real job when I was seventeen. It was during the summer before my senior year in high school. A friend of our family needed part-time help at his printing company. I didn't have a car, but it was close enough that I could ride my bike or one of my parents would take me if the weather was bad. I made a whopping $3.35 per hour (minimum wage at the time).

The first couple of days I put together notepads. I stacked sheets of paper, separated every so often with a piece of cardboard, into a vibrating machine that lined up all the edges. After they were straightened, I pulled the stack out and painted red glue on one side and left them to dry. I would go back later and cut the stacks into individual notepads and put them into boxes to be shipped to our customers. Sounds exciting, right?

After a couple of weeks someone quit and I was asked to help the print operator. My job included moving huge rolls of paper into position to print union newspapers. We used long "cheater bars" to lift the rolls into the end of the printer. I remember the sound of that big old machine cranking up. It started slow, but after a couple of minutes it was running full tilt and spitting out several twenty-to-thirty-page papers every couple of seconds. I stood at the far end of the machine to get the papers when they came out. I stacked them according to their destination and ran them through a machine that tied them with string into bundles. Then I pushed the bundles down a conveyer system where they sat until I stacked them onto pallets and moved them to the docks to be shipped.

As an official member of the 98 lb. weakling club, moving huge rolls of paper, running machinery, and stacking newspapers on a pallet was actually pretty cool. I felt like I was growing into a man.

Learning to be productive and taking care of myself was an incredible feeling.

Mom and Dad didn't have a lot of money to pay for all of us to go to college, but the expectation of college was there. If I wanted to go, I was going to have to figure out how to pay for it. I qualified for a work-study program and worked in the maintenance department at the college. I earned more than the money to help pay for my formal education. After cleaning a few bathrooms on Saturday mornings, after Friday-night parties, I learned I didn't want to do custodial work for a living.

During my sabbatical I began to think about work and how it has always been a part of my life. I also noticed Scriptures that talked about the benefits of work. There is a consistent principle in the Bible: Hard work is good and leads to God's blessings, which may include material benefits, but laziness is bad and you will go hungry. Today, there are a growing number of people who believe hard work and the material benefits gained are somehow bad. That position is not supported by Scripture. Working hard and making a lot of money is not sinful. Worshipping work and money, hurting others to get it, and spending it selfishly—those are all sinful behaviors, but working hard is a biblical principle.

People have tried to defend their anti-work, anti-money position by misquoting Scripture and stating, "Money is the root of all evil," but that is not what the Bible says. In 1 Timothy 6:10 it says, "The *love* of money is a root of *all kinds* of evil" (emphasis added). There is nothing wrong with working hard and gaining a lot of money from your work. We just need to keep it in the proper perspective. In its most basic sense, money is nothing more than a tool—a tool with value that can be used to provide what we need and want. It can be used to take care of others and advance God's kingdom.

Throughout Scripture, those who worked hard and did their jobs well are spoken of highly and blessed. On the other hand, those who did not work hard were criticized and suffered. Please understand, I am not saying that everyone in poverty is there because they are lazy or refuse to work. Many are there because of hard situations or they are Dont's and need to gain the resources, opportunity, and instruction necessary to care for themselves, but as a principle, Scripture puts the responsibility to work and provide for our own needs on the individual and not the circumstances. Several of the Proverbs show us what will happen to those who work and those who don't.

> *A man will be satisfied with good by the words of his mouth, and the work of a man's hands will reward him.* (12:14)
>
> *The slacker craves, yet has nothing, but the diligent is fully satisfied.* (13:4)
>
> *There is profit in all hard work, but endless talk leads only to poverty.* (14:23)
>
> *The one who is truly lazy in his work is brother to a vandal.* (18:9)
>
> *Laziness induces deep sleep, and a lazy person will go hungry.* (19:15)
>
> *The slacker does not plow during planting season; at harvest time he looks, and there is nothing.* (20:4)
>
> *A slacker's craving will kill him because his hands refuse to work.* (21:25)
>
> *Do you see a man skilled in his work? He will stand in the presence of kings. He will not stand in the presence of unknown men.* (22:29)

Obviously, working hard and working diligently are good things. While many of us have a love-hate relationship with work,

God didn't view work that way. God created us to work. He established work as part of His "very good" creation. Let's remember that "very good" means "perfectly perfect." God established work as a part of creation because He knew it was exactly what was perfect for humanity.

God created us with needs and desires that can only be met properly if we work. With the money gained from work, we can provide food and shelter. We can pay our bills. We can save for the future, our children's college funds, and refreshing vacations. We can support the kingdom of God and make His name known around the world. All these things are possible through God's gift of work.

That's right, work is a gift from God. While we use work to gain these things, God gave Adam a job before any of those needs existed. Let's remember, it was just Adam in the garden. There was nobody else. For all the single ladies reading this, please take note that God gave Adam a job before He gave Adam a wife. Do yourself a favor and follow God's pattern, but back to the point...

Adam was completely alone. He had no family, no need for protection, and food was literally hanging from the trees. He didn't need to save for retirement, buy his wife flowers, take her on a date, or save for his children's college funds. Adam was the only person on earth, and He was already a member of the kingdom. Since sin had not yet entered the world, there was no need for evangelism, discipleship, or caring for the poor, but God still gave Adam a job.

As you know, I began to ask a lot of questions about the Bible during my sabbatical. I began to wonder why God even created humans with needs in the first place. He could have made us with no needs at all, but He didn't. Why did He create us with a constant need of food and water? Why do we need shelter when He could have created the environment in such a way that we would not die from exposure? Why didn't he give us fur like other animals that would keep us warm during the cold and not cause us to overheat in the hotter months?

I continued with my questions. Why would God's perfect plan require us to work in the first place? What did Adam gain? Why was it so important? Why is work necessary? Why should we work to care for our own needs?

God could have provided Adam with everything. He could have created things in such a way that Adam would never have had to lift a finger, but He didn't. He created Adam, and the rest of us, with needs that could only be fulfilled with work. Work must be pretty important if it was part of God's plan for Adam before he needed it to gain the supplies required to live. If God gave Adam a job before he needed it to gain the necessities of life, then work must provide something even more essential than money.

As I prayed, continued to study Scripture, and reflected on my own life, I realized we gain a lot more from work than just an income. We gain things that money can't buy. We gain things that God made necessary for our well-being. We gain things that make us whole. We gain things God knew we needed to have a full life.

As I continued to reflect on my own experience, I remembered back to my first job. I had such a feeling of accomplishment. Then I remembered an even better feeling, my first paycheck. Do you remember that moment? I was on top of the world. I was so proud of myself. Not an arrogant, sinful pride, but a deep feeling of accomplishment. I knew I was being productive and becoming an adult.

As I have presented this material, I have asked audiences if they remembered their first jobs. I get head nods and smiles, then I ask about the first paycheck. Their faces light up as they remember that moment. It's amazing to me how many people remember that first check. It is a significant moment in our lives. I have had people in their seventies, eighties, and even nineties tell me exactly how old they were, how they earned it, and the amount. I've noticed the pride in their voices as they walk down memory lane.

That feeling of value isn't a mistake. God created each of us with a desire to take on responsibilities and accomplish things. He embedded a code in the DNA of every human being to meet their own needs. We want to be useful. We want to provide for ourselves. God gave Adam a job because he needed to believe he had value and was worth something. Relying on others to provide for our basic needs is a learned behavior.

We see the desire to care for ourselves in every child as they grow and find their identities. We see it in their desire to be independent. We even see it when they play. Most boys want to drive trucks and tractors and build. Most girls want to be teachers and nurses and care for others. While the examples may be stereotypical, it points to our natural desire to work, be productive, and have value. This desire isn't taught to children. It's given to all of us by God.

As adults, a large part of our identity is wrapped up in what we do for a living. When we meet someone new, it is common to ask where they work or what they do. That question may bother some people, because they don't think their work defines who they are, but I disagree. We find a large portion of our value and identity in our jobs. As we get to know others, it is perfectly understandable to ask what they do for nearly half of their waking hours. It isn't a bad question because it explains a major segment of our lives.

Our work, and our ability to independently provide for our needs, provides us with dignity. We find value in ourselves. God's plan allows us to see ourselves through His eyes as people who were created with abilities, purpose, and significance. We were created in His image. God calls us to work because He worked, and He has deemed work as necessary for our well-being.

I recently saw a post on a social media site from a single mother we work with. She has MS, which makes it hard for her to find and maintain employment. During the last twelve years, she has been in and out of work as the pain and ability to stay out of bed has gone up and down. She was doing very well with her symptoms and wanted to go back to work. We recommended her for a job and after she got her first paycheck she put up this post:

Making $$$ feels so good.

Now understand this is a woman who has her basic needs met through assistance from government programs, churches, and nonprofits. She has no real needs that have not been met through these services. Of course she has many wants that have not been met and she deals with a lot of inconveniences in her life, but she has everything she "needs." Yet she wanted to work. She wanted to feel useful.

This incredible feeling she had was because she earned something for herself. No one gave it to her. It wasn't a handout. It wasn't charity. She was living within God's plan. She had worth. Worth is the quality that renders something useful. It has intrinsic value that is nonnegotiable. She felt useful and it felt "so good."

Let me stress this again. The value and pride we gain when we grow and learn to provide for ourselves is not sinful. On the contrary, I believe it is evidence that God's plan exists and He finds value in us and our ability to care for ourselves. Misplaced greed and pride are sinful, but God created us with abilities and He expects us to use them, which in turn give us dignity. A major part of that dignity is found in our ability to work and independently provide for ourselves.

Working to meet our physical requirements is necessary to live, but we are more than just flesh and blood. To live as God intended us to, we need more than just food, shelter, air, and water. We have other needs. We were created as physical, emotional, psychological, and spiritual beings. These are the things that separate us from other animals. God's plan provided for all of these needs.

Dr. Abraham Maslow was an American psychologist who developed a theory about human behavior called Maslow's hierarchy of needs. He found five areas of human development. His theory was that as we meet the most basic needs, we naturally move up the pyramid to meet higher level needs. At the base are air, food, water, sleep, the ability to go to the bathroom, etc. These were categorized as physiological needs, which are necessary for humans, or any other animal, to survive. The next block on the pyramid are safety needs: resources, employment, family, health, property, etc. The third level is the need to love and belong: family, friends, and intimacy. The fourth is esteem: confidence, achievement, respect for ourselves, and respect from others. The top of the pyramid is self-actualization: morality, creativity, spontaneity, problem solving, and justice.[2]

Maslow's theory had five levels, but each of them can be placed into the four areas God created in us: physical, emotional, psychological, and spiritual. Dr. Maslow's theory weaves these four areas together into overlapping categories. As a humanist, Dr. Maslow didn't see the spiritual need in his younger years, but as he grew older he recognized the need to live for something bigger than ourselves. He criticized his own work and the highest need was found incomplete. So he added a sixth level entitled transcendence needs, which included purpose, spirituality, higher goals than our own abilities, and altruism.[3]

All of the needs identified by Dr. Maslow are fulfilled or enhanced through work. Our ability to provide for ourselves has a major impact on each of these areas. None of them exist in isolation. They are all intertwined. It is not possible for us to reach our potential without fulfilling God's plan and working to provide for our own needs. God gave Adam a job and calls the rest of us to work because He designed work to meet the needs of our entire person.

Now, people have told me I don't know what I'm talking about. They point out that I was raised in a comfortable home with two parents, I have little formal collegiate training, and I'm white. Those statements are all true. I was raised in a comfortable home, I do have two parents (who are still married today), I did leave school to provide for my wife and child, and I am white, but those facts do not change the truth. We have needs that can only be met by working and living within God's plan, and my life hasn't been a fairy tale. I've been there. I've struggled.

Meredith and I have not had the easiest road to travel. Yes, we both owned our businesses and lived very comfortably, but that was not how we started. We didn't have enough money to eat when we were first married. It was 1984, my sophomore year and her freshman year in college. We met in September, were engaged in October, were pregnant in January, and were married in May. We were two young, stupid kids who dropped out of college to raise another kid.

We got a job managing a sleazy motel near 28th and Division in a rough part of Grand Rapids, MI, but it included a two-bedroom apartment as part of our pay. Our best customer was a prostitute named Cookie. She was there when we took over and she was there when we left. We had thirty units; twenty-five of which were rented by the week or month. Most of the people who lived there probably should have been in some form of mental health facility where they could have received the help they needed. We were surrounded by drugs, gangs, and felons. We stayed there for just a few months until my oldest brother came to visit. He said, "Rob, this is no place for you to raise your child. You have thirty days to get out of here."

109

My parents had moved to Dallas, TX, and Meredith's were still in Michigan, and to be perfectly honest, we didn't want to live near either set of parents. We wanted to face life on our own. Nashville, TN, was in the middle and I had a sister who lived there. I knew she would help if we needed help, but would leave us alone to figure out life without interference. We moved to Nashville in September 1985.

I got a job at a landscaping company making minimum wage, which was still $3.35 an hour. With a $335 per month rent payment, plus utilities and a car note, there wasn't much left for food. Even if the weather held and I actually got forty hours each week, I had to work a hundred hours to pay rent, and that does not take into account the money paid in taxes. We lived off macaroni and cheese and popcorn. After a couple of months, I broke down and asked our church for help because we got the Cut Off notice from the power company. As much as I appreciated the help, it still bothered me and made me question my value and abilities as a husband and father.

Over the next several years we received help from government programs, nonprofits, and churches. Each time someone helped, it was another reminder that I was not doing my job as the head of our household. When Meredith checked out at the grocery store, I would not go with her if she was using food stamps, or I would walk away when she paid. It was humiliating. My confidence was shaken and I was tempted to give up.

Now I will be the first to admit I was full of a sinful pride and expressed it in negative ways, but I have seen the exact same feeling of failure in the eyes of many of the men and women we have served. I have seen the lack of confidence that they will ever break free from their poverty. I have seen their defeated reality that nothing will ever change. I have seen their despair. God's plan provides dignity, value, and a belief in one's own abilities.

In God's outline for caring for the poor in the Old Testament, all these things were provided through His instructions and the requirement for the poor to engage in God-ordained work to meet their needs. Our current programs and services miss these important aspects of humanity. Not only do they fail to fulfill these needs, but they actually do more damage than good. They tear down dignity, value, and confidence. These are replaced with a sense of worthlessness and uselessness in a hopeless people with no purpose.

Several years ago I was meeting with a young father whom I had been working with. He had been in and out of work for various reasons. He had a lot of reasons why he couldn't find and keep employment, many of which were self-inflicted because of his poor personal choices. At the time of this lunch, he had recently lost his job because of an issue with his manager.

We were finishing up and had already talked through most of what we covered on a regular basis when I stopped for a second, wondering if I should ask the next question. It was not a question I had ever asked anyone before. I knew him pretty well and didn't believe he would be offended. I also believed he would answer the question honestly. I had a good idea what the answer would be, but wanted to hear it firsthand. I wanted to confirm what God had shown me about His plan. So I took a deep breath and asked, "What does it feel like to live in the projects?"

His face fell. He was visibly uncomfortable. He adjusted himself in his chair, lowered his head, and fumbled with the drink in front of him. The question hung in the air for a few seconds, which felt like an eternity.

Maybe I had misread the situation. Maybe he was offended. He was certainly uncomfortable. I was starting to regret asking and began to think of ways to change the subject. Then, as he continued to stare at his cup, he began to talk.

"Man, you don't have to tell me I'm worthless. I feel it every day when I pull into the hood. Sometimes I drive by three or four times before pulling in, because of how dark it is in there. Living there is a constant reminder that I am not good enough. I am not good enough as a husband. I'm not good enough as a father. Every time I have to ask somebody to help pay my light bill or help us with food, it shows me that I can't do it. When the church stops by and they give my kids the Christmas I want to give them—it's just another nail in the coffin. I am not good enough. I am worthless."

His raw emotion shocked me, but his answer wasn't a surprise. His answer confirmed exactly what I had learned during my sabbatical. He vocalized what many in our inner cities feel. They don't feel worthy. They don't have dignity. They don't find value in themselves.

Our ability to provide for ourselves has such a significant impact on our lives. It helps us find our identity. It gives us a reason to get out of bed every morning. Teddy Roosevelt said, "Far and away the best prize that life has to offer is the chance to work hard at work worth doing."[4] I may not agree with everything that our twenty-sixth president said, but he did understand the importance of work.

God created us to work. He deemed work necessary even before it was required to provide for us physically. He created us with additional needs, which are essential to life and only fulfilled through work. Providing for our own needs gives us hope for our future and the future of our children. And hope is one of the main things missing from our inner cities.

DISCUSSION QUESTIONS

1. What are your thoughts about work based upon the example you experienced growing up?
2. How did you feel about yourself the day you got your first job?
3. How did you feel the day you got your first paycheck?
4. Can you remember your first job, how much you made per hour, and the amount of your first check?
5. What are the negative effects of giving people things they should provide for themselves?
6. How are we cheating people out of a God-designed value by providing things for them that God intended for them to provide for themselves?

CHAPTER 8

APPLICATION

Now it's time to get serious. We have covered the what—the Four Fundamental Elements. The who—the Can'ts, the Don'ts, and the Wont's. The why—the dignity, value, and self-respect earned through caring for our own needs. So far, we've established an understanding of God's plan to restore broken people. We're halfway home.

Now we get to the hard part. This is where we begin to struggle through the application. We still have to use all of this information as we serve in our communities and around the world. We have to cover the how, where, and when. This is where the rubber meets the road. They say that "the devil's in the details." Well, we're about to get knee-deep into the details, but I hope you can see it's from God and not the devil.

Some of this may sound divisive, but division is not the intention. The intention is to boldly and clearly share the truth of God and how we are called to represent Him to a lost and broken world. I pray you do not feel attacked, but I will not sugarcoat the facts. I believe we have become so accustomed to our Christian leaders spoon-feeding us messages we want to hear, and completely skipping the application, that we get offended by the truth. I pray that if you are offended, you are offended by the message and not the messenger. Before we move forward you may want to recite the prayer that started my sabbatical and we began this journey with, *Lord, show me Your heart*, because applying God's heart to our lives is often painful.

We live in a microwave society. We don't like to wait. We want things fixed and we want them fixed quickly. We rarely spend the time investigating to discover the underlying reasons behind behaviors or situations. If a child's behavior is not acceptable, we want immediate change, so we give that child a pill.

Some friends of ours have tried a new approach to training their son. When he disobeys, talks back, or is rude, they stop, try to calm the situation down, and then ask, "Where is your heart right now?" They want to get to the reason behind his behavior. They want to get to the cause. This question has led them to some incredible conversations about how we represent Christ in our everyday lives.

Our desire for the quick and easy fix has also infiltrated our service to the poor. Most of the time, energy, and money spent is focused on the symptoms of the struggle. That's not what Jesus did. Jesus always addressed the reasons and not the results of the struggle. Jesus didn't give away clothes, set up food pantries, or establish homeless ministries. He healed people, because if the cause is corrected, then the symptoms take care of themselves.

God's plan treats the cause and not the symptoms. I learned that Meredith and I had previously served with methods that did not address the cause. When we helped set up food distribution days and gave away 20,000 lbs. of food at a time, lack of food was just a symptom. When we delivered Christmas gifts to kids, kids not getting a gift at Christmas was just a symptom. We were only focused on the symptom and did nothing to address the cause.

Many churches and organizations provide felt-needs services with no strings attached. Their understanding of the Bible leads them to believe that requiring something from those in need does not represent Christ's heart for the poor. As we learned in chapter 4, they are wrong. Their actions go directly against God's plan. We have to learn that love does the hard work. Love does what is right and not what is easy or feels good.

Some of you who provide felt-need services may be getting a little hot under the collar right now. I completely understand how you feel. I have been there. I have felt that same level of frustration when I realized the largest part of my service was improperly focused. I appreciate your belief that you have identified a problem and are devoting your life to meeting that need, but please stay with me.

Before I am labeled a heretic and people are calling for my head, let's set the record straight. Felt-need assistance must continue to be available. Scripture requires us to provide for people who are physically or mentally unable to provide for themselves. It's necessary to deliver services to people who live in areas of the world where the land cannot produce enough food and water for those living there. We also need to offer assistance to those who are going through hard times, but this must only be available as a stopgap measure.

I am not saying that providing these services to hurting people is a sin. They are necessary, but they must be done in the right way and with the right motives. Doing something poorly is often worse than doing nothing at all. The systematic, long-term provision for people who are physically and mentally capable of caring for themselves must stop. It must come to an end. These services have a detrimental effect on everyone and in no way display the love of Christ. If your service has a singular focus on the symptom, are you really meeting the need? Or are you adding to the problem?

Case in Point—Meredith's Back Pain

To better understand this, let me step away from ministry and use a medical example. For several years Meredith had been struggling with chronic back pain. Thankfully, we have found an incredible chiropractor who utilized a holistic approach to medicine that includes chiropractic care, diet, and exercise. Meredith was seeing him on a regular basis because of her problem. Although the adjustments helped, he kept telling her that adjusting her back was not enough. Though she had short-term relief, the problem continued.

He told her there were underlying issues causing her continued pain. He asked again and again if she would be willing to go through some dietary testing, but she refused the tests. She just didn't want to spend the money. She kept living in agony and kept making trips to his office. Meredith and I tried all kinds of things to eliminate the pain.

We bought a special pillow, but that did nothing. She tried inserts for her shoes, but they provided little relief. Looking back, I think we could have funded the ministry if we had taken out stock in pain-killers. She was getting ready to go out of town in April 2011 and stopped by his office on a Tuesday for her regular adjustment before her Thursday flight. She left his office and, as usual, was feeling quite a bit better.

That evening we went out for dinner and had Italian. I don't remember if we were celebrating something or if we were just having a nice dinner before Meredith left. Either way, we ate like crazy. We had mozzarella cheese, pasta, bread and more mozzarella cheese and more pasta and more bread. We had more carbs and dairy than any two people should eat. We had sodas with refills. We even ordered a dessert. We ate as much food as we could possibly fit into our bodies in one sitting and went home to fall into a food coma.

Meredith woke up the next morning with the worst pain she had ever experienced. She was unable to walk. It started in her hip and was shooting up her back and down her right leg. She could not put any pressure on that leg. She headed back to the chiropractor's office that Wednesday morning and told him he had one day to "fix her" because she was going out of town. He told her the adjustment would not help and asked if she was finally willing to let him look at her diet. She agreed and he ran some tests.

We soon learned Meredith's body was not able to properly process certain types of food. We found out she has a dietary intolerance to gluten, corn, dairy, egg whites, and peanuts. Everything we had eaten the night before was wrong. She had literally been poisoning her body with her food choices. Our entire diets had to change.

It took us a few months to get used to the changes, and the first time we went to the grocery store, Meredith cried as we read label after label on the items we normally purchased and ate. It took us three hours to find food for the next two days. It is difficult finding foods that have none of those products, or any by-product of those products. Let's just say we stick to the outer edges of the grocery store now. The point is, Meredith's diet was the cause of her back issues. Although we had identified the pain as the problem, it was just a symptom of her body's inability to properly process certain types of food.

Today, Meredith goes to see our doctor about once every six months. She has lost over 50 lbs. without doing anything other than changing her diet. She can take long rides in the car without pain. She has more focus and energy, and feels so much better. All because we identified the root cause of the problem.

She was willing to go through the testing to better her health. She was willing to make the necessary changes to end her pain. She could have kept going to the doctor and kept downing pain-killers and caused even more damage to her body. Instead, she discovered and dealt with the cause. I hope you are already getting the point of this and can see how it relates to ministry.

If we applied many of our programs and services to Meredith's situation, this is how we would have responded: We would have used our benevolent funds to pay for her medicine. We would have found a doctor in the church to donate a special pillow, specifically designed to reduce the pressure on her back. We would have continued to spend money on shoe inserts and the chiropractor, but none of those things would have ended the problem. Treating the symptom never ends the struggle.

Case Study—Lambscroft Ministries

We partner with an organization here in Middle Tennessee called Lambscroft Ministries. Lambscroft Ministries reaches out to the homeless and operates a shelter a couple of nights a week. Each Wednesday and Saturday you will find them serving eighty to a hundred men. They provide the same services as a lot of other shelters, but they go beyond merely giving a hot meal and a place to sleep. They give the men an option to change their lives. This is done in two ways.

First, they offer transitional housing to men who come to the shelter, but want to get off the streets. The Discipleship Houses address some of the basic struggles these men face. They have a place to shower, shave, and get cleaned up. They have a contactable address to put on an application while they search for employment. These men are given the support services they need to get back on their feet, but the services offered by Lambscroft don't end there.

Second, Lambscroft has a restaurant, called The Cookery, which they use to provide culinary training to men who are looking for a way to end their cycles and get back on their feet. They learn how to read recipes, proper knife skills, and food presentation. Not only do they learn the art of cooking, but they can also learn how to operate and manage a restaurant. They make incredible food—from scratch. The community is rallying around the business and the men are gaining the Four Fundamental Elements.

Lambscroft is not completely unique. There are other shelters that offer the same types of assistance. The difference with Lambscroft is their founder, Brett Swayn. Brett moved to Nashville in 2002 with a very common story. He was going to chase his dreams and make it big in the music business.

Like a lot of these stories, life didn't go the way he planned. Brett lost everything and ended up homeless. While living on the streets of Nashville he learned the unique struggles of the homeless. He experienced the heartache, alienation, and desperation. He calls this period the "hardest, most beautiful time" of his life, because he experienced a closer walk with God and came to understand the sufferings of marginalized people in America. As Brett tells it, "My life changed through a series of miracles." He got a job at a high-end steakhouse with locations all over the country. He worked hard, learned the craft, and became a sous-chef. He was soon traveling around the country, training others in the culinary arts.[1]

Brett could have donated large sums of money or given a lot food to the homeless. He could have gone on the circuit, telling his story and bringing awareness to the reality of homelessness, but that's not what God called him to do. He left his career to invest in the lives of the homeless and poor. Brett knows the root of the struggle. He's been in their shoes and experienced it firsthand.

Brett is a living, breathing example of God's plan for restoration. His life changed because he treated the cause and not just the symptoms. While homeless, he faced the problem of hunger, but it was a symptom and not the cause of his struggle. What Brett needed were the resources, opportunity, instruction, and relationships necessary to care for his own needs. It has come full circle and today he helps others break free from their bondage so they can care for themselves.

Focusing our service on treating symptoms has unintended consequences. If Meredith had continued to take pain-killers, her liver could have shut down. If Brett had been given food instead of a career, hundreds of men would still be lost in cycles of addictions. Focusing on the symptoms does more damage than good. We are breaking the people we are called to serve.

The Heart of the Matter

Let's get right down to it. Why are we serving? Do we actually want to make a difference or just make ourselves feel good? If we are called to make a difference, then we have to be willing to do the hard work and do what is best for those served. It's not easy. What is best often doesn't feel good. Does it mean we do not feed the hungry? No, we are clearly told in Matthew 25 to feed the hungry, clothe the naked, and visit the suffering, but I think the Matthew 25 passage may be one of the most misinterpreted parts of the Bible. Let's put it into context.

Jesus tells three parables in that chapter. The parable of the ten virgins, the parable of the talents, and then the parable of the sheep and goats. In the first two parables, those who were not prepared to meet their own needs were punished. Jesus was clearly not calling us to blindly give things to people in the third parable. We must understand it is possible to serve the poor improperly. First Corinthians 13 is the love chapter and tells us that we can, "give away everything to the poor and offer my body to burned," but if it is not done as an act of God's love, it is useless. Blindly giving to the poor is not a display of God's love.

I think we all can agree on a couple of things. We all believe everyone is created in the image of God. I don't know any Christian who would argue with that. I don't think anybody is going to disagree with the idea that everyone has purpose, abilities, and potential. Well, if we can all agree that these two things are true, why don't our services reflect this belief? Why don't we serve others with their value, purpose, abilities, and potential in mind?

I will never forget the day that Laura was born. Amanda was facing the challenge of being a single parent, but she was not going to face it alone. She had a support system around her and asked her two sisters, Meredith, and me to be in the delivery room with her. Amanda's water broke at 7:30 in the morning on May 16, 2008. It was a very long and exhausting day and I wasn't even the one in labor.

At 9:52 that night, through screams and tears, Laura made her appearance. They wrapped her in a blanket and handed her to Amanda. The rest of us pressed in to see our new family member. Much to my surprise, Amanda held her for only a few seconds and then handed her to me. I was going to be the man in Laura's life and Amanda wanted me to spend some of those first few moments with Laura.

As I stared down at this incredible gift from God, I was overwhelmed. I felt an area of my heart I did not even know existed jump to life. I felt it begin to fill with a love I had never experienced before. It was nothing short of amazing. Is there anything more miraculous than the birth of a child?

This young life had been created in the image of God. I whispered a prayer in her ear. I prayed for her protection. I prayed for her future. I prayed she would grow into an incredible woman of God and live for Him.

I prayed for strength to be the man who would lead her. I prayed I would give her an example of how a godly man treats a woman. I prayed I would know how to point her to Jesus. I committed to sacrifice my own desires, comfort, and security so this young child would have every opportunity afforded to her. I promised to do everything within my power to help her become the woman God had created her to be.

Today, as I look into the eyes of the men, women, and children we serve, I wonder what their birth was like. Did someone hold them and appreciate the incredible miracle of that moment? Did someone find a new place in their heart they did not even know existed? Did that moment change someone else's life forever as they prayed for that child?

Do we see this kind of value in those we serve? Meredith and I have a long history of serving, but I have to admit I did not always see those we served as unique creations made in His image. I often missed their value. I thought I was there to fix them. Thinking I would simply ride in on my white horse to relieve the suffering of the poor, I had a savior mentality.

You may think this attitude doesn't apply to you and you may be right. It may not, but you know this attitude is alive and well in churches and service organizations. We serve out of pity, not because we see value. We want a quick solution so we can feel like we've done our part and go back to our lives. We want to be able to check the box.

We hear of a single mom who can't make her light bill, so we write the check because, *That's what love would do.* We find out there are a group of men living under the bridge and we give them blankets when it's cold. *You know, Jesus said when you give to the least of these, you've given to Me.* Blindly providing for the needs of others is not a display of godly love. In fact, I don't think it is a display of any form of love.

If serving others by addressing the symptom is a display of love, then I owe my children a huge apology, because I obviously hated them. You see, I taught them to work hard. I pushed them to be the best they could be, to display character and integrity, and to succeed by living a godly life. That's what parents are supposed to do. That's what love does.

I don't think any parent wants to see their children struggle. I can't speak for anyone else, but I would move heaven and earth to help my children regain their footing if they fell on hard times. I would help with immediate needs, but I would pour even more resources into a solution. We would do what was necessary to overcome the cause. Only meeting the situational need does not represent God's heart, but that's what most of our services do.

When people ask how they can be involved with Against the Grain, which happens often, we offer them several opportunities to develop relationships and equip people to better handle the challenges of life. Their response often goes something like this: *Oh...don't you just have a service project we can do to help you out? Maybe we can do a food drive or collect diapers? Do you all do Christmas for the kids or need help delivering Thanksgiving baskets?* They want to treat the symptom, but aren't willing to help overcome the cause.

John Perkins is a man who has devoted his life to the service of others. He is a pioneer in fighting for justice and equality. In his book, *With Justice for All*, he writes, "There are two reactions to poverty and injustice—social service and social action...Social service takes a food basket to a needy family at Christmas; social action tries to eliminate the conditions which produce the hunger."[2] John Perkins understands God's plan for the poor. We must invest in solutions and give people a future.

Several years ago, Rick Warren wrote a book that had a major impact on our society. People ran to stores to buy it. He was featured on news program and talk shows, and his face graced the cover of magazines. His book became the topic of Sunday school classes, life groups, men's and women's small group studies, and retreats. His book is still in the top 50 list of all-time best-selling books.

Why did this book take the country by storm? Why did more than thirty million of us buy it? People put other books aside and even took days off of work to read this one. What did he share that was so important? Was it a fail-safe secret to financial success or a guaranteed method for raising our children?

No. It was none of those things. He showed us there is a reason we are here. He led us to find something bigger than ourselves, something that motivates us to get out of bed every morning. We found significance. We discovered we were put here for a reason. We learned our lives were not a series of random events—we were created with a purpose.

If finding our purpose is so important, why don't we want to provide that same opportunity to those we serve? Isn't it important for them to discover their purpose? Don't they deserve the privilege of getting out of bed every morning knowing they were created in the image of God for a reason, or is that only for us? Either we don't see they have purpose or we don't care that they have one. It has to be one or the other. If we see their purpose, then we must help them work towards that purpose. Our service has to provide more. No one's purpose is to stand in line for a box of food.

Without a sense of purpose, people can fall into addictive, self-destructive behaviors. A lack of purpose can cause stress on relationships. Marriages can be destroyed. Children can be abused. A lack of purpose affects every area of our lives.

People leave their jobs for all kinds of reasons. It may be their boss. It may be the pay. Some may be moving and others just want a change of scenery. There are thousands of reasons why people choose to leave their jobs.

I found a lot of top (5, 8, 7, 10) reasons why people leave their jobs. It is possible there are as many lists as there are people with opinions on the subject. Reading the lists got a little boring because most had the same basic reasons. While the lists changed the order of importance, there were three or four consistent themes: mean boss, not appreciated, and not enough money. After these three, each report had additional reasons for leaving.

A bad boss, not being appreciated, and lack of income all seem to be pretty valid grounds to seek new employment.

There was one other reason consistently given in many of the studies: "I did not feel like I was able to use my abilities and talents." These people felt that they had a contribution to make to the team and were unable to do so because they weren't properly using their abilities. If these lists are correct, then being able to use our abilities and talents is important. We all want to use our gifts and talents.

God certainly thought they were important. We learned in chapter 3 that He called people who had specific abilities and used them for His work. When the children of Israel were building the sanctuary and all the furnishings to be used in worship, God called those with specific abilities. In Exodus 28 God tells Moses to *"instruct all of the skilled craftsman, that I have filled with a spirit of wisdom, to make Aaron's garments for consecrating him to serve Me as priest."* In chapter 31, God names Bezalel and Oholiab as men to whom He gave specific abilities to build the sanctuary.

Do we see the abilities of those we serve? Do the programs we offer allow them to identify and use their talents? Do we encourage, even require, them to use their gifts to care for themselves? Our services must change and provide a pathway for them to grow. No one properly uses their abilities by walking to the mailbox to get their support check.

We have to begin to see the potential in those we serve. A person's potential speaks to their future. The word *potential* can be used as an adjective or a noun, but always refers to the qualities, abilities, or capacity that will lead to future success or usefulness. Potential sees possibilities. Potential sees a reason to go on. Potential knows there is hope for the future.

Is there anything more depressing than believing you have no future? Meredith and I have had several opportunities to speak in juvenile development centers and to high school groups over the last several years. Most of these young adults have been involved with the legal system. It is sad to hear how many of them are already defining themselves by their juvenile mistakes. They don't believe they have any value. They don't see their potential. They have very little hope for the future.

When we speak at juvenile centers and in jails, we don't see the people by their records. We don't define them based upon their past. We see their value. We see their potential. We see future plumbers, electricians, CEOs, teachers, and business leaders. We see doctors, lawyers, pastors, mothers, and fathers. We don't see convicts, screw-ups, or charity cases. We see them through God's eyes.

Have you ever heard someone described an "EGR" person? I hadn't until one day after serving in the community. A church asked us to partner with them for an event in the projects because a family who attended their church lived there. They believed God was calling them to be more active and wanted to develop relationships with this family's neighbors. We explained our services and God's plan for restoration, and they were excited to join us in the effort.

Overall, it was a pretty good day. After the event we were invited to join them for dinner at the local Mexican restaurant. They began to "debrief" over chips and salsa and had a wonderful time. As we were leaving I asked about the family who attended the church and mentioned they had not joined us for dinner. The pastor's wife looked at me with a grimace on her face and replied, "No, we didn't invite them. They're EGR people. They just don't fit in with us."

I learned that EGR means Extra Grace Required. This family had different backgrounds than everyone else at the church. They didn't have the same level of education, they didn't run in the same circles, and they didn't shop at the same stores. I was thankful we were climbing in the car when I heard this news. We do a lot of prison ministry, but I have never wanted to do it from the inside as one of the inmates.

This group did not see the value in those they served. They did not see God's image in that neighborhood. They saw them merely as a project, a way to check a box to prove they were relevant. They did not display God's love. They only treated symptoms and never addressed the causes.

We must represent God's plan for the poor. We must stop using all of our resources on the symptoms only. It is time that we reevaluate our services and begin to address the root causes of the struggle. This will require a new approach to ministry. This is done by helping others gain the Four Fundamental Elements for themselves.

I asked God to show me His heart and He did. His heart is to show the poor they have value. His heart is to let them find their purpose. His heart is for them to learn they have abilities and potential. We are called to be His hands and feet and take this message to the lost and broken in our world.

DISCUSSION QUESTIONS

1. What negative ways of serving the poor have you seen?
2. Meredith had to go through the painstaking process of finding the cause of her pain. What are some of the consequences of treating the symptoms and not the cause?
3. How did Brett Swayn's experiences in life prepare him to better serve the homeless?
4. How will our services change if we find the skills and abilities of those we serve?
5. How important is it to help hurting people find and fulfill their purpose in life?
6. What are some ways you can show the poor they have value and help them gain dignity?

CHAPTER 9

GUIDING PRINCIPLES

When we began to work with the moms and were establishing our services, we wanted to follow a complete, biblical structure of caring for the poor. We wanted to represent God's plan. We wanted to treat the causes and not the symptoms. We wanted to take all of this information and put it into practice. We did not take this process lightly. We prayed and continued to seek God's heart.

As we applied all of this to ministry, Meredith and I were encouraged as we saw the women begin to make real changes in their lives. We started to see the results of God's plan. We were loving and, more importantly, He was restoring the broken. The women were gaining confidence and beginning to realize their abilities, value, and purpose. They began to see themselves through God's eyes.

Even with all these positive signs, Meredith and I battled our old habits. We often wanted to step in and take control. We heard heartrending stories and would go to bed at night and weep over the pain shared that day. There were many times we thought it would be easier to rescue the women. We were tempted to return to our old way of doing things.

We struggled to stay focused on God's plan for restoration and quickly realized we needed to create some guiding principles around the services we offered. We needed to ensure that God's plan was represented properly. We had to go against our instincts and follow His lead. To help us work through each unique situation, we established Four Guiding Principles, one principle for each of the Four Fundamental Elements.

Fundamental Element #1—Resources

As we know, God made resources available for people to take care of themselves. While He made them available, He did not deliver them to the front door of anyone's tent. God provided the resources, but the people had to go out and do the work. This truth applies to meeting everyday physical needs as well as responding to God's call to perform specific tasks. We need to help those we serve gain the necessary resources on their own.

God provided everything Noah needed to build the ark, but Noah had to do the work. He had to cut the trees and haul them back to the work site. The children of Israel were given manna and quail in the desert, but they had to go out and pick it up. Everything needed to build the tabernacle came from material blessings the Israelites had received from God. Throughout Scripture God made the resources available, but He required people to have a stake in the process. He didn't give resources, He provided access to resources.

Guiding Principle #1—Never give what can be gained

When our girls were in high school we, like every other parent, made the dreaded annual trip to the mall to get all the clothes and supplies the girls needed for the upcoming year. By the way they shopped you would have thought we had a money tree in the backyard and could pick off as much as we wanted anytime we wanted. They walked into every store and asked for all the latest trends and fashions. After a year or two of nearly going broke trying to keep our girls up with the Joneses, we changed our system. We gave each of our girls a hundred dollars, which they had to work for, and we told them they could keep all the money they did not spend.

The girls, who had previously wanted everything, suddenly became super shoppers. Our oldest decided the clothes she had were good enough and kept the entire hundred dollars. The other two spent some of the money, but they weren't interested in buying the hottest name brands. In fact, they went straight to the clearance and sale racks. They ended up buying a lot of clothes at thrift stores. What they were interested in buying and the way they treated their clothes was entirely different when they invested in the process and had something to gain from being good stewards.

On the other end of the scale, we had a young lady stay with us for a few months while her mother was in jail and rehab. The first night she was there, Meredith asked her to set the table for dinner. She stacked five glasses on top of five plates, with the silverware thrown into the glasses, and began awkwardly clanking towards the dining room. She wobbled back and forth trying to keep the "leaning tower of housewares" from crashing to the floor. "What are you doing?" Meredith asked as calmly as she could. "You can't carry all of that at once. What's going to happen if you break them?"

The young girl seemed surprised. She replied, "It's no big deal. Someone from a church will come by and give us new ones." Meredith's heart sank as she explained that it doesn't work like that. Nobody was going to give us a set of dishes. If we broke them, we would have to buy new ones.

Now I don't blame the young lady for her understanding or her reality. In her life experience, if the dishes broke, some "kindhearted" person would just give them more. The problem is that this young lady had not learned the importance of taking care of things. The dishes had no value because they didn't cost her anything to receive or replace. Have you ever noticed you appreciate something more when you purchase it with your own hard-earned money?

Requests for material assistance were a common thing in the beginning of AtG. Many people asked us to give them things they needed, anything from clothes, to diapers, to schoolbooks so they could gain an education. We would tell those who asked that we won't "give" them things, but we would help them gain these things for themselves. With a smile we told them, "If you earn it, you own it."

Many organizations have an Earn While You Learn program. The program may utilize something as small as a closet packed with household items or as big as a thrift store with everything people need. Participants can earn credits or Program Bucks by showing up to class, doing the homework, or achieving new levels of independence, and they can use those credits to purchase things from the store. We have used this model and have seen the pride gained by earning something rather than getting it for free.

A church put this policy into place with their benevolent funds. They were known in the community as the church that would pay your bills and had a constant stream of requests. They also had a lot of tasks volunteers performed around the church. The leadership had learned that handouts were humiliating, encouraged irresponsible behavior, and did not represent God's plan, so they established a new policy. The church would continue providing financial assistance to the community, but would require recipients to help with the volunteer needs. It was necessary for those requesting funds to make an investment and earn the money. There would be no more giveaways; the recipients had to work for it.

The Monday morning after the new policy was put into place, a regular recipient of funds showed up asking for help with her electric bill. The pastor told her they would be more than happy to help, but she needed to volunteer six hours at the church. She was a little confused and asked what he meant. He told her their policy had changed and they weren't just going to give her the money, but would give her the opportunity to earn ten dollars per hour and that money would be used to pay the bill.

Boy, was she angry. She couldn't believe it. She got loud and wanted to argue, but the pastor held his ground. As she left, she told him she was "going to go back to the neighborhood and tell everybody that this church hates the poor." The pastor felt terrible, but was committed to following God's plan.

A few days later a young lady walked in the church office and asked if the pastor was there. He came out to meet her and she said, "I hear you all will help me if I do some work around the church." The pastor explained the policy and she asked what they needed her to do. She helped clean up the sanctuary and folded some bulletins. The church paid her bill. She thanked them and left.

A month or so later, the same young lady came in and told the pastor her power was about to be cut off. She wanted to know if they needed work done around the church. He said they did. She did the work and the church paid the bill. She thanked them and left.

The next Monday the same young lady came back again. She told the pastor, "I have a bill that is going to be due next week. Could I do some work now so I don't have to worry about it later?" He commended her for planning ahead and told her they would be more than happy to help. They gave her some jobs and she went to work.

The staff was scheduled to have lunch together that day. One of them suggested they invite their new friend. She was embarrassed and declined. She told them she didn't have the money to pay, so they told her it was their treat. She was visibly uncomfortable, but they assured her the church was going to be paying for everyone.

Over lunch they heard her story. They heard about her struggles. They heard about her two young boys. They soon returned to the church and she finished her work. Around three o'clock, she went home to get her boys off the bus.

Thirty minutes later, this young mother walked back in the door. She had brought her boys with her. She wanted to introduce them to the staff. She kept saying, "These are the people I've been telling you about." Her excitement was obvious; it was written all over her face.

Long story short, this young lady began attending the church. She joined both the church and a life-group. She accepted Christ and was baptized. They helped her find a job from a business owner in the church, and today she is proudly taking care of the needs of her family.

This young mother's legacy changed when the church treated her with love instead of seeing her as a charity case. She had lived off the system since childhood, but this church's service changed her life. She is living with dignity. She has accepted Christ and joined the church because they followed God's plan. She wanted to serve a God who loved her enough to give her value.

Fundamental Element #2—Opportunity

God provided for the poor, but He didn't do it through handouts. He never established systematic programs to care for those who were able to care for themselves. He gave them opportunities. He gave them a chance, but they had to act. God didn't do it for them.

God provided opportunities for the poor to get food. He told the Israelites not go back over the fields twice, but to leave what was left for the poor. The Israelites were not to pick up what had fallen to the ground so the poor could come and gather their own food. They were given the opportunity, but the choice was theirs. God wanted them to work for what they received.

Guiding Principle #2—Only do for others what they cannot do for themselves

This takes work. This requires us to get to know those we serve. We have to identify what they are able to do for themselves. We have to know if they fit into the category of the Can'ts, the Don'ts, or the Won'ts. We have to know their strengths and weaknesses and learn if we are treating a cause or symptom. We provide opportunities, but opportunities come with responsibility.

Let me give you an example. We have all seen the TV shows where people get their homes updated or made over for various reasons. Meredith and I love those shows. We judge the quality of each episode based upon whether one or both of us cry when the bus is moved and the home is unveiled. There are some incredible stories of people who struggle for various reasons and the community rallies around them.

Maybe a child was born with a disability and the parents can't afford to update the home. There have been veterans who have been injured and needed changes to maintain independence. Most of these shows feature people who work really hard and have had life-changing situations. The shows are heartbreaking and redemptive. These programs show us the power of a community that loves and cares for each other in positive ways.

With the success of these shows, there are churches and service groups that want to get in on the action. They want to provide makeovers in their own communities. They put out feelers, pick a recipient, and go to work. It may be as simple as a cleaning project, it may require some home remodeling, or it may be anywhere in between. They show up on a Saturday with cleaning supplies, tools, and truckloads of new furniture.

Out with old and in with the new. They work all day and have an incredible time. When the family returns after a day of being spoiled, everything has changed. New paint, new furniture, a fridge full of food, and new plates on the dinner table. Tears are shed, thank-yous are given, and everyone goes home with sore backs, warm hearts, and enough memories to last a lifetime.

A few months later someone from the church decides to stop by and check on the family. They are invited in and can't believe their eyes. How can this be? What happened? The house looks just like it did before their work.

It's a wreck. The floor can't be seen under all the trash. Dirty, stained, and chipped plates overflow in the sink. There are holes in the walls. The furniture is soiled and snagged. All that work was done for nothing.

Now there is nothing wrong with cleaning a home. Some people need the help. We have cleaned a lot homes for the elderly and disabled. The Housing Authority comes through twice a year to inspect and make sure the units are being taken care of properly. We provide assistance before the inspections to those who can't do the work themselves.

It's a hard lesson to learn, but people must be responsible for their choices. They have the right to live the way they choose; therefore they have the right say no to assistance. We don't get opportunities alone. With an opportunity comes responsibility. If someone chooses not to take responsibility for their life, then we must stop rescuing them from the consequences of their choices.

We have a saying that communicates this to the men and women who work with us. "We will invest in you as much as you are willing to invest in yourself." If they are not willing to do the work to have a clean home, then we are not willing to clean it for them. We will give them the opportunity and may be willing to help in the process, but at that point the burden of responsibility shifts to them. We are not responsible for their choices.

We receive requests for job referrals on a regular basis. People call and ask for a lead or to use us as a reference on an application. If this person has not shown that they can be responsible with the opportunities they have received, then we will not agree to vouch for them. We are not going to put our names on the line for someone who doesn't follow through on their commitments. If they can't show up to class, why would we believe they could show up to work?

When we provide an event instead of an opportunity, we are usually treating the symptom and not the cause. Doing for others what they can do for themselves makes them feel incompetent. By giving them the opportunity and responsibility for their own care, they begin to believe in their abilities. They begin to realize they have value. They begin to understand they can make a difference. They begin to see themselves through God's eyes. Guiding Principle #2 shows them they are capable.

Fundamental Element #3—Instruction

God never gave an opportunity without the necessary instruction on how to accomplish the task. We find this example in the garden when He gave Adam the rules and taught him how to work the ground. Remember that God did this before the fall. This means Adam cared for the garden before there were weeds that had to be controlled so they didn't choke out the food. God gave Adam the opportunity and made sure he had all the instruction to perform the task.

Guiding Principle #3—Teach, don't take over

We invest in what we believe in. When we don't teach, we are communicating that we don't believe they are capable of doing things for themselves. They don't gain confidence and they don't believe in their own abilities. Doing for others, instead of teaching them to do for themselves, creates a pattern of reliance upon the giver. Our services have to teach others to care for themselves.

We are never told to take-over someone else's care. Everyone I have ever talked to agrees with the "give a fish, teach to fish" philosophy and while it sounds easy, it is hard to put into practice. Most organizations give instead of teach. Very seldom is teaching others the purpose of our services. In most cases, we do for others instead of teaching them to do for themselves. This must change.

Here is a quote from one of our moms when she was frustrated with a program offered by one of the local churches. "If we don't know how to do something...*teach us*! Don't call us stupid and do it for us. Why would I go to a church that tells me God loves me, and then abandons me, rejects me, or controls me when they find out I'm not that easy to help?"

I'll be the first to admit it's easier to *do* than *teach*, but usually the easy answer is the wrong answer. When our kids were in school, Meredith and I had a constant battle. The kids would sit down with their homework and look to us for help. Meredith would read the question and either provide the answer or find it for the kids.

This drove me crazy. She wasn't teaching our children to figure things out for themselves. She wasn't helping them in the learning process. When I pointed this out, she said, "I don't have time to show them how to do it." She took the easy way instead of the right way.

This situation came back around shortly after we started AtG. We had a mom who enrolled in college and needed help with her English papers. We decided that I would be the one to work with her. She came over each week and I helped her with the assignments. I stood in the room and talked her through the papers, but she did the writing. I didn't do it for her. I taught her how the writing process works.

Each week she called to tell us the grade she had received on her papers and we reviewed them. We talked through the professor's comments, learned from them, and applied that information to the next paper. I was able to help her write every paper that semester, except for one. The dreaded final exam. She had to do that one in class, on her own.

We waited patiently—OK maybe not so patiently—for her grade to be posted. We called her every day or two looking for an update, but she hadn't heard back. A week or so later she stopped by with the news. She wouldn't tell us the grade she had received until we heard the whole story. She wanted us to know what had happened.

The professor gave her the prompt and two hours to write her response. She froze. She had writer's block. She tried to put the words on paper, but they just wouldn't come. She got frustrated and wondered what would happen if she walked out of class. Then she thought, *How would Rob write this paper? What would he ask if he were standing right next to me?*

After that the words began to flow. She got her paper done and turned it in. She made a B+! Her confidence level shot through the roof. She knew she had the ability to do college-level work.

God calls us to help others become the people He created them to be. We have to devote our time and energies into helping others grow in their own abilities. We must invest our resources in equipping. Our purpose is to teach them how to meet their own needs. We provide the instruction, but they must do the hard work.

When we don't teach those we serve how to independently care for themselves, we communicate our lack of faith in them. It doesn't matter how many times we tell them they have abilities and are loved. As the old saying goes, *Your actions speak so loudly I can't hear our words.* Our actions have shown them what we believe. We have made them feel worthless.

When we invest our time and resources in their abilities and teach them, they begin to gain confidence. They begin to believe in themselves. They feel they are loved. They grow in the knowledge that they have abilities and can do things for themselves. They know they have value.

Fundamental Element #4—Relationships

It's all about relationships. All ministry is relational. People need to know you care about them. As Theodore Roosevelt is often attributed with saying, "People don't care how much you know until they know how much you care."[1] God created us to have relationships with others and commands us to love others the way we want to be loved.

Guiding Principle #4—We will love our neighbor as we love ourselves

When I began dating Meredith, I had a purpose. I knew pretty quickly I wanted to spend the rest of my life with her as my bride. I wanted her to know I would always have her best interests at heart. It was important for her to believe that I would protect her. I wanted her to understand that I would serve her.

Meredith and I are complete opposites. While I am almost always hot, she will wrap up in a blanket on an eighty-degree day (I have pictures). I like things put in their place and she likes an organized mess. I like small group conversations and she likes being right in the middle of a large crowd. I'm a night owl and she likes to go to bed early.

Meredith hits the floor running the second she wakes up, but I don't really get moving before 9:00 a.m. I had heard there was a special breed of people who liked mornings, but I wasn't sure I had ever met one of these odd folks. Meredith, the woman I wanted to spend the rest of my life with, turned out to be one of them. She wakes up with energy, ready to face the world. She is a morning person.

Meredith and I met while we were in college. She had a job in the cafeteria on campus and had to walk roughly one-half of a mile to get to work. I lived in an apartment in a different area of the campus, approximately a mile from her dorm. She helped prepare and serve breakfast, which meant she had to be to work at 5:00 a.m. (That's right—for the love of all that is good in this world…5:00 a.m.?)

I didn't feel comfortable with her walking across campus alone at 4:45 in the morning. So I left my apartment at 4:30 and jogged to her dorm. I walked her to work, then jogged back to my apartment to try to get some sleep before my 10:00 a.m. class. I wanted her to know I was serious about my commitment to protect and serve her. I was willing to sacrifice my own comfort to make sure she was taken care of.

While I "took care" of her by walking her to work, I didn't tell her to quit her job. She needed to work if she was going to stay in school. I looked out for her and encouraged her, but I also pushed her to do her best. I knew she could achieve great things. This meant I had to have some hard conversations with her. I talked with her about areas of her life that needed improvement. In the same way, she talked to me about areas of my life that needed improvement. This is a practice we still employ today, because that's what love does. Love is willing to go through the uncomfortable, awkward, sacrificial moments for the benefit of the one they love.

Love does what's right. It does not look for what is convenient or easy. Love wants the best for the object of that love. God calls us to love our neighbor as we love ourselves, but what does that mean? In Luke 10, we read the parable of the Good Samaritan. This story was given as Jesus' response to an "expert of the law," which starts with the following interaction.

> *Just then an expert in the law stood up to test Him, saying, "Teacher, what must I do to inherit eternal life?" "What is written in the law?" He asked him. "How do you read it?" He answered: Love the Lord your God with all your heart, with all your soul, with all your strength, and with all your mind; and your neighbor as yourself. "You've answered correctly,"*

He told him. "Do this and you will live." But wanting
to justify himself, he asked Jesus, "And who is my
neighbor?" (Luke 10:25-29)

The lawyer wanted to justify himself. This is why Jesus told the story of the Good Samaritan. You may be familiar with the story, but let's hit the highlights for those who aren't.

A man traveling down the road between Jerusalem and Jericho was attacked by robbers and left for dead. Soon, a priest came down the road, then a short time later, a Levite came down the road, but both of these men did nothing. Well, that's not entirely true. They actually did worse than nothing. They crossed to the other side of the road so they didn't potentially become "unclean" in case the injured man reached out and touched them. Talk about looking down on someone and not seeing their value as being created in the image of God.

Then a Samaritan, who was considered a social outcast because he was half Jew and half Greek, saw the man and took action. He bandaged him up, poured oil on his wounds, put him on his donkey, took him to a hotel, and cared for him. Being a responsible man, the Samaritan had to go back to work the next morning, but he wasn't going to leave the injured man alone. He told the innkeeper to finish patching him up, with the promise that he would return and fully pay the expenses for the wounded man's recovery.

Jesus asked the lawyer, "Which of these three do you think proved to be a neighbor to the man who fell into the hands of the robbers?" Now, this is a smart guy. He is an "expert of the Law" after all. Of course, he said it was the Samaritan (the one who showed mercy). Jesus congratulated him on his correct answer and told him to go and do the same.

There are all kinds of good lessons we can learn from this passage. We can learn that a job at a church does not mean you represent Christ. Maybe the "take-away" is that having position, power, and prestige doesn't mean you're going to do the right thing. We can also learn that the knowledge of God doesn't mean you put it into practice. While all of those are important lessons to learn, there is something else I want you to take away from this story.

The point I want you to see is the Good Samaritan provided more than just common decency. He didn't just give the guy some bandages, bread, and water. He didn't drop him off at a shelter and say, "Hope you get better, have a good day." He didn't merely throw money at the situation. He didn't start a petition, organize a march, or launch an awareness campaign to bring attention to the dangers of the road between Jerusalem and Jericho.

Rather, he served his neighbor. He sacrificed his time, money, and experience. He did for the injured man what he would have wanted someone to do for him. He loved his neighbor as he loved himself. But how do *we* do that? What does that really mean? What does it mean to love our neighbors as we love ourselves?

The truth is, we don't apply "love" to those we serve in the same way we provide it for those we truly care about. Instead of saying, "love your neighbor as yourself," why don't we say, "love the hurting as you would love your own child"? This brings a new twist to the way we think about loving our neighbor, but this viewpoint has been helpful to me as I consider our responses to the requests for services we receive. What would be my response if my own children were in need of help? How would my goals for serving them change? Would there be requirements, limitations, or boundaries I put on the assistance?

Would there be time frames established? Would there be any requirements attached to my help? Would I hold them responsible for their actions? Would I insist they work toward finding a solution to the situation? Would there be the possibility of discipline if they didn't follow through?

I would probably do all of the above, and even more, if I wanted to be a good parent. A parent's job is to train their child in the way they should go. We raise them to represent the legacy of our families and, according to Hebrews 12, love includes discipline. Sometimes, love is displayed in ways that don't feel loving. It is called tough love for a reason.

Tough love doesn't give us the "warm fuzzies." It takes effort. It makes the hard choices. It sacrifices its own broken heart for the long-term benefit of the one loved. That is the heart we need to begin to display to those we serve.

We must see them as the unique beings that God created. We must help them identify their purpose, use their abilities, and achieve their potential. We must help them gain the Fundamental Elements for themselves, and we must do all of this with love. We must do what is best for their long-term benefit. We must serve them with their future in mind. Love brings hope to the hopeless.

DISCUSSION QUESTIONS

1. What are some of the positive and/or negative effects of not giving something that can be gained?
2. Why are we so interested in doing things for the poor instead of investing in them and giving them the tools necessary for them to do things for themselves?
3. What happens to people who are constantly provided for and never taught the skills necessary to care for themselves?
4. How does empowering others and equipping them to care for themselves display love?
5. How does relieving personal responsibility display a lack of faith in someone's abilities?
6. What are some practical ways we can serve others with their future in mind?

CHAPTER 10

DOMESTIC MISSIONS

Over the last thirteen years, Meredith and I have seen a lot of what does work and what doesn't work. We've learned to respond with the Guiding Principles and introduce people to a Jesus who cares about them on this side of eternity. We've done some things right and we've done some things wrong. Each time we've taken those experiences and tried to learn from them. It's tiring, frustrating work and the greatest thing we have ever been privileged to experience.

We've seen people break generational cycles and change the legacy of their family. We've seen others reject God's plan and run back to their old ways. We have tried to serve in ways that helps others find their dignity, value, and purpose through a personal relationship with Jesus Christ. We've led atheists to Christ and baptized people in swimming pools. I even got to baptize (wrestle) a woman with an incredible fear of water. We have seen people who were running from God embrace Him as their Savior.

We've also learned to say *no* to a lot of service opportunities. We will not add to the pain and struggle of those we serve. We will not be a part of a service that makes things worse. Over the next few pages, I am going to share some of our experiences and some of what we have seen. Let's look at a couple of the "what not to do" stories.

A Broken Ministry Model

One thing we did to help the moms get back on their feet was provide childcare if they were going to work or school. We were doing this for one of the moms who could walk to work, but she didn't have transportation to bring her kids to us. We arranged to pick them up before she left for work and take them back after her shift. This arrangement caused us to be in the neighborhood, and more specifically at her home, a couple of times a day. It also allowed us to get to know the people who lived on the other side of her duplex.

One afternoon we stopped by as her neighbors were sitting on the front porch laughing and having a great time. I said hi as usual and then said, "Man, y'all sure seem to be having a good time today." The wife responded, "Yeah, we are. We just got a church to pay off all our bills. Four thousand dollars to be exact." The husband laughed and said, "Yep. We'll never see them again. That's OK. I don't have to go to work tomorrow." He ended up losing his job, they couldn't afford their rent, and they lost their apartment a few months later.

If this example needs a lot of explanation, then I have done a really poor job of communicating God's plan. This church made matters worse. They didn't give this family value. They didn't give them dignity. They didn't build relationships or point them to a loving Jesus. Our service should not remove someone's God-given responsibility to care for themselves.

This man had a responsibility to care for his family. He had a job and could make the payments. They weren't being taken to court and they weren't losing their apartment, but the church stepped in and took over. They did not follow God's plan. They undermined this man's ability to be the leader of his family.

150

Let's look at a common scenario we have seen several times from churches that want to introduce themselves to the community. They don't know how to make the introduction so they decide to throw a party. Understand, I believe their motives are pure and not all parties are bad. They want to be the hands and feet of Jesus. They really do have good intentions.

The church establishes a committee and they start planning. They pick the date and the theme. They decide this is going to be the block party of all block parties. Flyers are made and volunteers walk through the community to personally pass out the invitations. It's going to be a great day.

There will be inflatables, face painting, and games for the kids. There will be basketball, football, and contests for the teenagers. The men of the church will bring their grills and cook hotdogs and hamburgers. The women of the church will make desserts and have bingo and cake walks. The worship team will play some music and the youth will run the kids' area. There will be drawings for gas cards and grocery store gift certificates. To top it all off, at the end of the day, everyone who is there will get to take home a huge box of food.

The day is unbelievable. It goes off without a hitch. There isn't a cloud in the sky, the humidity is low, and the temperature is glorious. Everything works perfectly. The people from the neighborhood show up in huge numbers. Some of the kids from the church know some of the kids in the community from school. There are screams of laughter as they run and play together.

God miraculously multiplies the burgers, dogs, and chips and there are even twelve boxes of food leftover, which jokingly reminds them of the time Jesus was feeding the crowds. There is a great sense of joy as everyone packs up and heads home. The video, shown the next morning in church, is set to the perfect music and brings a lot of smiles and a few tears as people remember an absolutely incredible day. They really were being the hands and feet of Jesus as they served the poor. It could not have turned out better.

In the takeaway meeting, held the next week, everyone agrees the event was a huge success. The only downside was the number of people from the church who couldn't attend because of soccer leagues and vacations. The committee talks and decides to move next year's event to the fall so even more people will be able to attend. The budget committee agrees to double the amount for next year and allocates $4,000 for the event. All of the games, music, and food will be expanded. On top of that, backpacks and school supplies will be given away. There is such a fire and excitement in the church. It is unbelievable how good it feels to serve the Lord.

Now let's think through this scenario from a different perspective. For this exercise to work, you are going to have to help me. I want you to try to get inside the mind of a single mother in poverty. You have to try to grasp the reality this mother faces every day. While it's impossible for us to truly understand, I'll paint a pretty clear picture. These are not made-up scenarios, but are based on the actual stories of people with whom we have worked. To start, I need you to set aside your current understanding of the world and try to walk in another person's shoes for a few minutes.

Life has been very hard. You have never had much. The dice have never rolled in your favor. There have been a lot of nights you have gone to bed hungry. Your home is hot in the summer and cold in the winter.

You can't afford window A/C units. Even if you could, they would possibly be ripped out of the windows and stolen. You can't keep your home warm enough in the winter so, every night when you go to bed, you turn on the oven and crack the door open to provide a little extra heat in the apartment. The TVs and radios are always turned up loud, and you have to yell to talk to your kids, but the noise from the electronics is better than listening to the screaming and fighting you hear from the other side of your thin walls.

You are in a continuous state of anxiety. Nothing is guaranteed. You have no reliable form of transportation. Your friends and family will help with rides, but they always want something in return. If you don't have money to pay for gas, they will take payment in food stamps. Or, if you get a ride from a man, he may want something a little more intimate as payment for taking you to the pharmacy to pick up your child's asthma medicine.

You have never really been successful at anything. You always dreamed of moving out of the projects, but life just didn't work out that way. When you were young you thought an education would be the answer, but no one from your family had ever graduated from high school and your mom couldn't help you with your homework. That one time you did bring home the report card with all As on it, it wasn't hung proudly on the refrigerator door, but thrown in the trash with an accusatory question, *Are you trying to be better than me?*

All of your friends are in the same situation. You don't have many examples of people who have been lucky and actually "made it." You can't trust anybody because your own family will steal your tax refund if they get the chance. The only people you know with extra money are the drug dealers, and the only ones not living in a constant state of fear are in the gangs. Overall, life sucks. You have no education, no job, no future, no real friends, and no hope.

Now this may sound like an exaggeration, but these are fairly common occurrences. These are a combination of actual stories told to us by the mothers we have worked with. I remember the first time I saw a mother throw a good report card in the trash and an oven used to heat the house. It didn't fit into my

153

understanding of the world. The comment about a son or daughter "being better" than a parent has been repeated more times than I can remember. I have realized a few things that helped me understand why someone would say this to their child.

When I was a kid, my parents wanted me to do my best and perform at the highest level. When I disobeyed I heard, *Kendalls don't behave like that.* My parents always pushed me to continue the legacy of our family. There was a standard I was expected to reach and was encouraged to go even further. I have seen that this family pattern can also work in reverse for families in generational poverty.

The mother's legacy is doing what is necessary to get by. Please understand, I'm not blaming anyone or saying people in poverty are useless or weak. In fact, most of the people we work with are stronger emotionally and mentally than I will ever be. What I am pointing out is the importance of family influence and beliefs. How did we learn to interact with the world, and what were the expectations put on us in our childhood?

Now let's look at this same block party from the other side of the equation. One day, while sitting on your porch, you see someone walking through the neighborhood. They look nice enough, but you wonder if they're a social worker coming in to take someone's kids. You start to get nervous as they walk up to your unit and hand you a colorful flyer about a block party. You can't really read it, but the nicely dressed person standing on your porch fills you in with the details.

We are going to have a party in the community this Saturday. We are going to have a great time. We'll have blow-ups and face painting for the kids, games and contests for the teenagers, five grills going with burgers and dogs, and everyone who comes will be entered into drawings. At the end of the day, we'll be giving away boxes of food. It's going to be amazing! Remember...it's this Saturday. Hope to see you there.

The idea of a block party doesn't excite you. You're not really interested in going, but you haven't had a burger off the grill in a while. You have nothing better to do. Who knows, maybe it will be fun. You talk to the neighbor and decide to go together.

Your expectations are pretty low. You've seen these types of events before. You get up Saturday morning and walk down to the party. You play games and talk with people, accept the box of food, and say thanks. The day turns out to be better than you thought, but soon the group is packed up and gone and the neighborhood quickly returns to normal.

You sit in your apartment lonelier than usual. The fighting next door, over who gets the extra hotdogs that were sent home, is just a reminder that life hasn't changed at all. You heard some of the people talking as they were getting in their cars and know they are going out to dinner to celebrate a fun day of serving. The mom next door screams for the boys to "shut up and go outside!" because she has a headache and is tired from the day in the sun. You are left with a confusing mix of emotions.

You're truly thankful for the food and you did have some fun, but the gas card you won won't help because you don't have a car. Of course, you can use it to pay for a ride the next time you need to go somewhere. All the attention made you feel uncomfortable. You don't like hugs or being touched. The only time anyone has ever told you they loved you was when a guy wanted something.

The entire day just confirmed that you are exactly what you believed about yourself. You are a charity case. An uneducated, unemployed, hopeless person with no future and who can't do it on her own. You are unable to provide for yourself. You aren't good enough. You are worthless.

Now this may sound harsh and it may have made you angry as you read it, but I have been in the community when the party is over. I've seen the letdown and I've have heard the comments after everyone leaves. *Well, that was fun*, someone says. *Guess we won't see them again until next year.*

Yeah, another replies. *That's if they actually come back.*

I sure hope they feel good about themselves. You know, helping us pitiful little ol' poor folk.

We must change the event-based programs that do nothing more than make us feel good. We must make a difference in our communities. Event-based programming is transactional. The entire event is based on one party giving and the other party receiving. These events create the hierarchy that builds barriers and separates us. God did not call us to transactions. He called us to relationships, but relationships take effort. Relationships are hard and we can get our hands dirty.

Let's be willing to try some new approaches to ministry. Does your social service, church, or nonprofit provide people with one of the Four Fundamental Elements, or do they perpetuate the degrading cycle of giving things away? Why don't we teach a mother how to budget her food stamps instead of giving her a box of food? Why don't we use our church kitchens, which sit empty the majority of the year, to hold cooking classes. Why don't we teach people how to care for their communities instead of holding an annual cleaning day? How degrading would it be to have outsiders come in with trash bags and clean up your community?

Before working through the block party story, I told you that I believe our motives are good. We want to be the hands and feet of Jesus and our hearts are in the right place. While this is often the case, I have also seen a selfish side of ministry. Let's take the mask off and be real for a couple of minutes. We don't want to be burdened with too large of a commitment. We want to make a difference, but we want to serve Jesus on our terms.

Now before you get too defensive, there is a minority of churches, nonprofits, and individuals who are working within God's plan. There are those who provide job skills, life skills, and tutoring assistance as well as present the gospel in real ways. It's not all bad news. There are groups, both domestic and overseas, that are fighting to end the causes of poverty at the very root of the problem and provide dignity to those who are being served. They are providing the Four Fundamental Elements and they are changing lives, but those organizations and services are few and far between.

On the other hand, the majority of our programs only meet the immediate need. This has to change. All of our services need to be transformed and reflect God's plan. Unless there is a commitment from those who need assistance, and a plan set in place to help them become independent, their request for assistance must go unmet. We have to gain the courage and take the time to figure out how to respond. We have to identify which of the Four Fundamental Elements are missing and then tie any services offered to them working a plan to gain those elements for themselves.

Lessons Learned

Meredith and I have done our best to follow God's plan and anytime we strayed from that plan, it has come back to bite us. I know this won't shock you, but things never seem to work out well when we don't do them God's way. We have made a lot mistakes. We have learned what works and we have learned what doesn't. We have had success and we have had failure.

When we begin to work with a new person at AtG, we start with an interview process. It's not super formal, but it allows us to get to know them. We get to hear their story. We learn their strengths and weaknesses, and we hear about their dreams. We identify the Fundamental Elements they have and the ones they are missing. We develop an Individual Life Plan (ILP) to keep all of us focused on helping them achieve their dreams.

Transportation is a vital resource as people struggle to get back on their feet. On several occasions people have donated vehicles to be given to the men and women we serve. We distribute this resource, but we don't give what can be gained. The recipient is required to meet some basic standards to earn the vehicle. Here are the stipulations:

1. Cars are given away on a first-come, first-served basis.
2. Recipients must be working on their ILP to stay on the list.
3. The car will be given away, but the recipient must have money for the vehicle inspection, registration, license plates, and insurance. (We will not pay those fees.)

Almost every experience of giving away a car has turned into a success story, but we aren't perfect. One of the most painful events we endured began when we got a call from one of our partner churches. They found a mom, with her three daughters, on the side of the road and had already put her up in a hotel for the night. They wanted to know if we would talk to her. We picked her up and took her to dinner so we could hear her story.

She was a young mother escaping from an abusive husband. Her latest beating, which had happened the day before, was because there was no beer in the house. When he left to go to the store, she decided to run. She grabbed what little cash she could find in the house, her three daughters, and got on the first bus leaving town. That bus just happened to be heading to Nashville, TN. By the time she got here, after a long night on the bus, her husband had emptied all of the money out of their bank account, and she was broke. As we talked, we learned that she had most of the Fundamental Elements.

- *Instruction*
  She was a cosmetologist, but would need to transfer her license to Tennessee.
- *Opportunity*
  She could get a well-paying job if she were able to get her license transferred.

- *Resources*
  None
- *Resources needed*
  - Housing
  - Transportation
  - Food
  - Clothing
  - Cosmetology equipment
- *Relationships*
  The church that found her and our support systems

We reached out to people in our network. Another local church that provides short-term housing agreed to put her up in a motel. It wasn't the best place for her and her kids, but it had a small kitchen area and provided for the immediate need. We arranged for clothing and some food to be donated. With the immediate needs taken care of, we could begin to focus our attention on some short-term solutions.

We put out a plea and received an incredible response. Most of the remaining needs were going to be met by a group of women from one of the local churches. They helped with more food and clothing and agreed to walk with her as she got back on her feet. They even committed to purchase hair-cutting equipment for her when it was needed. The only thing left was transportation and long-term housing.

A couple of days later we received a call because someone wanted to donate a vehicle for us to give away. We made the decision to break our own rules and give priority to this new mother over the mom who had maintained all of the stipulations and was at the top of our list. Our new friend had no money so we paid for the inspection, plates, and registration. We even paid for the first installment for her insurance. She knew she would be employed by the time the next payment was due and offered to pay us back when she was on her feet. She was well on her way to establishing her new life in Tennessee.

She was genuinely humbled by the incredible response. She had never received any type of assistance and this experience was a little overwhelming for her. All the attention made her feel uncomfortable because she wanted to be able to care for her children by herself. She was not used to people helping her with babysitting and schedules and providing the necessities of life. She seemed to be heading in the right direction, but within a week or two we started to see a few red flags that made us question the truthfulness of her story and her desire to work and care for her family.

She began putting off the important things that needed to be done for her to become self-sufficient. She did not want to get a part-time job because she would just have to quit soon. She then started asking to be given more things. She missed her appointments to work on her resume and was very vague on where she had worked and how long she had been cutting hair. She kept delaying because she felt like her "life was in such chaos" that she could not concentrate. We made the tough decision to hold her accountable and no additional assistance would be given until she showed us she was serious about getting her life in order.

We talked with the women's group and they agreed to the new plan. They would not provide any more assistance until she began to work her ILP. The young mother went silent. We did not hear from her for a few days. We reached out to the women who had been walking with her and found out they had continued to provide support. Not only had they continued to help, but they had committed to provide even more resources.

In an attempt to inspire her to get her cosmetology license, they had presented her with thousands of dollars of brand-new hair equipment. They understood her feelings of chaos, so they agreed to cosign a one-year lease on a home. All the furniture had been donated and they were moving her in that weekend. They were going to fill the refrigerator with food and the closets with clothes. They had given her everything—she had done nothing to help herself.

A few weeks later we were driving through her neighborhood and noticed that her house looked empty. We checked with the women from the church, but they had not seen or heard from her. We asked around and found out that she and some guy had backed up a trailer, loaded up everything that had been given to her, hooked her car to the back, and left town. It was her husband.

She was not abused. They had been doing this in other areas and we were just their latest victims. In her wake she left a couple with months' worth of rent payments. The worst part of the experience is that many of the women who had invested their time and money will be reluctant to help anyone again. It was a bad experience all the way around.

Now here is the other side of this story. When we gave this mother the car, we put her ahead of the other young mother who was at the top of the list. She had been working and kept her job for a few months, even though transportation was always a struggle. She often paid nearly half of her day's wage or bartered some of her food stamps to get people to drive her to or from work. There were a few times when she walked the three miles from her apartment in the projects to her place of employment in bad weather, but she was not going to quit. She was determined to work hard and provide a better life for her daughter.

Later that summer we got a call from a couple with a vehicle they wanted to donate. This mom was finally going to get her car. We asked if she had the money for all of the costs associated with inspections, plates, registration, and insurance. She not only had the money, but had set it aside nearly four months earlier and had not spent it. With everything in place, she got her car.

Several years later, she is still driving that car. She keeps up the maintenance with oil changes and has replaced the tires. She continues to work her job, where she has received raises and promotions. She moved out of the projects and into her own apartment. She is setting the example for her daughter that hard work and discipline pay off. In three generations she is the first person in her family to move out of the projects.

These stories show what happens when we don't follow God's plan. We made the mistake of giving the first car before this mother had a chance to prove herself. The women from the church gave many more things as incentives when they should have held her accountable. She didn't earn it and we all got burned.

The second car was earned. She got a job, kept the job, saved her money, and proved she could be responsible. She is a shining example of what happens when we follow God's plan. God's plan does work. We just have to be willing to do our part.

DISCUSSION QUESTIONS

1. How well do you know the unique challenges that face the poor as they try to break the cycles of poverty and care for their own needs?
2. What are some of the ways you have been involved in serving?
3. How do you think those you served felt about your service?
4. What legacy has your family left for you to fulfill?
5. What are some ways you can help provide the Four Fundamental Elements to hurting people in your community?
6. How does requiring someone to have the money to pay for inspections, tags, and insurance help ensure they can take care of a vehicle?

CHAPTER 11

INTERNATIONAL MISSIONS

U p to this point, we have applied all of this information exclusively to Stateside ministries. We have reviewed God's plan in the context of our own services, in our own organizations, in our own hometowns, but we can't stop there. God's plan for people to provide for their own needs is not limited to domestic work alone. His framework to restore the poor will work in every situation. It can be applied across every setting. God's plan is timeless and universal.

If we are really interested in presenting a loving God to a lost and hurting world, then our international ministries must go under the microscope as well. We have to struggle through some hard questions. We have to be honest with ourselves even if we don't like the answers. We have to know if we are properly representing Him in our service to Third World countries. We have to discover whether we are healing or breaking the broken.

One of my goals in life is to be a man who speaks the truth in love, but there are some realities of our service to the poorest of the poor that makes it very hard to be loving. Sometimes, the godly response includes a little righteous anger. This may be one of those times. The previous chapter may have hit home and even offended some of you. Maybe you got your toes stepped on. Be ready, that was the easier of these two chapters.

Let me start by saying that I understand the appeal of taking a mission trip to a Third World country. I have had the joy of going on two of them and look forward to going again. I've been through the emotional highs of signing up, writing support letters, and getting my passport. I've gotten my shots, scheduled vacations, and packed my bags. I appreciate the impact these types of trips can have. It's incredible to travel to exotic places that challenge all five human senses and know it is all being done in the name of Christ.

I got my first taste of foreign missions in Haiti in December 1983. I was a senior in high school and spent my Christmas vacation serving. It was an amazing experience. The team from our church worked on a construction project. We added onto a small building that could not hold the number of people who showed up to church every week. It was hard work and was done side by side with the locals. It was an eye-opening experience for a seventeen-year-old who thought he knew everything.

While the work we did was important, there were some other lessons I learned that have changed my life. I realized that I bow to the idol of my own comfort, security, and selfishness. This lesson was learned as I watched the selfless act of a ten-year-old young man dripping in sweat from working in the hot sun. Our leaders thought we deserved a treat for our hard work, but this young man only took a quick taste of his ice-cream cone before handing it to his little sister as he returned to continue working while the rest of us finished our break. I am ashamed to admit that I had not thought of giving my ice cream to anyone.

When I asked about this young man and his sister, I learned the harsh truth of their existence. This ten-year old and his little sister were orphaned a year earlier. They lived in a box behind a store down the street from the church. Thankfully the pastor's family and local merchants looked after them, but at night they were all alone. He worked harder than any of us for the right to earn his small pay. He was determined to sacrifice his own comfort for the benefit of his sister. He worked to provide so she could go to school and gain an education.

I learned the realities of spiritual battles and that our enemy is real. I remember riding down an old dirt road in the back of a pickup truck. We kept passing what appeared to be parties going on back in the woods. We could hear the beating of the drums and the screams of laughter in the distance and saw the shadows of people dancing around the fires. It was a shock to learn that those were voodoo ceremonies and the drums, screaming, and dancing were accompanied by the ritualistic sacrifice of animals as they worshipped their satanic god. It was both exciting and terrifying at the same time.

I have also experienced the closeness of God. The power of His presence. I have learned to pray for my brothers and sisters in Christ. I learned that there are those who face life-threatening conditions as an everyday, normal part of life. I understand why we take these trips.

I will never forget standing on a bluff overlooking a lush green valley that was home to a quiet winding river in the Dominican Republic. The mountains off in the distance were a beautiful backdrop to the setting. The sun was bright and there was not a cloud in the sky. It was a scene that should have been featured in a magazine. The article could have been entitled "A Magnificent Display of God's Glory." It was absolutely amazing, but the view was more than my mind could comprehend in that moment.

Fifty feet behind me was a small block building with a metal roof and a dirt floor. I had just walked out the back to look at the property and see if there was room for an additional building to add an area to train the adults in skills that would allow them to provide an income for their families. The seventy-five children sitting inside that small block building were packed closely together on benches and plastic chairs. The announcements had ended and they were singing songs of worship before the children were given a plate of rice and beans. This was a good day because the group we were with was able to secure some chicken, which had been added to the meal.

This entire event was taking place in a village that had no building standards I was familiar with or had ever seen before. The homes were built of cardboard, blankets, and scrap pieces of wood. There was no electricity or running water. The kids were about to eat one of the two meals they were guaranteed each week. The disparity was more than I could comprehend. I wept as I tried to get my mind around the contrast of God's beautiful creation in front of me and the horrific living conditions behind me.

While I appreciate my experiences, I have to ask some hard questions. Are these trips effective? Are we providing the Four Fundamental Elements? Are we representing God's plan and making sustainable differences, or are we doing what feels good to us, but actually increasing their pain? Well, there is some good news and bad news as we review our international services.

The good news is there are some amazing organizations doing incredible work. They are meeting the immediate felt need while working on long-term solutions. They are serving in ways that keep families intact. They are providing opportunities for the Four Fundamental Elements to be gained. They are giving dignity and restoring lives in the name of Jesus.

The bad news is there are other, very familiar ministries that don't offer these benefits. While we think they represent a loving God, they are missing the mark. There are unintended consequences of our service that we may have never considered. They don't offer hope and actually move those we are serving even farther away from God's plan. The problem is that some of these responses are so entrenched in our Christian heritage that they seem to be untouchable.

We don't we want to test their effectiveness. We don't want to think through the hard questions. We don't want to deal with the pain, but if we are going to represent Christ and bring hope to the hopeless, then it is vitally important to take a hard look at these ministries. We have to answer this question. How are we serving the millions of orphans around the world?

Does our service cause more damage and deepen their pain? Are we properly investing in their lives? Are we getting a good return on the resources? Are we solely focused on symptoms when we should be devoting a much larger portion of our time, energy, and other resources to finding solutions? We have to wrestle through the truth of this work.

Why are trips to orphanages so attractive? Why do we spend billions of dollars taking short-term mission trips to work with orphans in Third World countries? When I think back on my trips, I have to ask if I gained more than they did. We must have the courage to review our work and be willing to kill the sacred cows.

If we are really honest and think critically through these trips, we may find there are selfish benefits. We will see that many of these trips are the ultimate in consumer Christianity. They are often more about us than they are about those children. They offer the perfect event-based response to a problem with none of the downsides. We are able to take an exciting vacation and feel good about doing it.

While many people take these trips with a pure heart, there are others who use them to insulate themselves from the most important of the Fundamental Elements; Relationships. These trips meet our needs on an emotional level, but are often lacking in substance. We get to travel, serve for Jesus, check the box, and go home knowing we have done our part. There is no long-term commitment. It is safe ministry that makes us feel good.

We get all the blessings and none of the curse. We get to see and experience things we have only dreamed of. We get hugs and pictures with the peace of mind that this child will never share a classroom or ball field with our own children. If we really wanted to serve children and show them Jesus, why aren't we doing it with the 108,000 orphans in the U.S. or the 400,000 U.S. children without a permanent home?[1] We have had volunteers refuse local work and take a mission trip because they didn't want their children around "those kids" in their own community.

If we had the best interest of orphans in mind, we would find a better use of our resources. Roughly 1,600,000 people took a mission trip in 2005.[2] I don't want to exaggerate the numbers, so let's say the average trip costs only $2,000. If the numbers remain the same, that means we spend more than $3,600,000,000, every single year, to go into other parts of the world and "love" people in the name of Jesus. That's 3.6 *billion*. Considering that 2.1 billion people in the world live on less than $3.10 a day,[3] I think our priorities may need to be reevaluated. Would you agree that there may be a better way for us to invest in their lives?

Now, many of us have taken these trips and may not be ready to accept their shortcomings. You believe you were there with altruistic motives and the above statements do not apply to you. That may be true. You may serve locally. You may have an overwhelming desire to see these children in your own community. You may be currently working towards adopting, or have already adopted a child and given them a loving home, but that doesn't relieve you of any responsibility. So let's ask some other questions about these trips.

Are they effective? Do our services provide dignity? Are we focused on providing the Four Fundamental Elements? Are we addressing causes or symptoms? Are we actually making a difference? What are the unintended consequences from our visit? These are the questions I cannot escape and they keep me up at night.

Both of the trips I went on were with the "good news" organizations. They utilize local leaders. They provide life skills training and microlending opportunities. They ensure medical care and education is available. They are easing the symptom while addressing the cause in ways that provide dignity, but many of our trips to orphanages don't have these benefits.

We make the necessary arrangements, pack up all of our materials, and head overseas. We want the children to know Jesus, so we hold VBSs and do crafts. We play games, give hugs, and love on the children. We smile for the pictures and cry when it's time to go home. Our lives are changed and so are those of the children, but we may find that most of theirs are not changed for the better.

Our trip did not help them. They were not better equipped to face the harsh realities of life when they leave the orphanage. We did not help them gain resources, opportunities, or instructions. Above all, we actually hurt their ability to gain the most important Fundamental Element: Relationships. Let me use Meredith's childhood experience to give you an example of this reality.

Meredith's family moved a lot when she was a child. She attended four different elementary schools and one of those schools she attended at two different times during two different school years. Those five school changes included six different home addresses between kindergarten and sixth grade. Some of them happened during the school year after she had established relationships with her teachers and classmates. Every year or so, Meredith had to say goodbye to her school and friends and develop new relationships with a new teacher and new friends at a new school in a new neighborhood.

This set a pattern in place which Meredith still struggles with today. She has a very hard time developing solid, long-term relationships with people outside of our immediate family. It's a defense mechanism that keeps her from going through the trauma of having to say good-bye to people she loves. Children in orphanages struggle with this same problem, but obviously their struggle is significantly greater than Meredith's. Each week these children quickly develop deep emotional ties with volunteers and then the volunteers leave in a wave of emotion.

Of course, this only adds to their pain. Every week new volunteers show up to love on them and their hopes of getting out of the orphanage are dashed. They are left alone with a hopeless reality. They learn that they get a lot of attention from strangers, some food, a bed, and the possibility of an education, but what they don't get is the consistent love, care, and attention that is only possible in a family setting. Over time, these children can develop attachment disorders and are no longer able to engage in healthy, loving relationships.[4]

But they don't have the option of families, I've been told. *Their parents all died from AIDS or were killed in wars*, others have said. While this is sadly true for some of these children, this is not true for the vast majority of orphans. According to research by Save the Children 94% of orphans in Indonesia are not actually orphans, but have at least one living parent,[5] and a 2010 study showed that only 12 percent are orphaned due to AIDS.[6] The truth is that four out of five orphans worldwide have one or both parents still living.[7]

Many of these parents were raised in orphanages themselves and don't know how to operate in a family setting. They have no skills or the ability to provide for their children. They see an orphanage as their best option. Others hope to provide their children with a free education, which is only available through an orphanage. Some are migratory workers who drop their children off while they travel to work in other areas of the country. Many of these parents return months later to find that their children are no longer there because of the ruthless, immoral behavior of the leaders in some of these orphanages.[8]

Are we really showing these children Jesus? Are we preparing them for a better future? Are we helping them find their purpose? Does our visit really give them hope? We come in to show them love, but leave them with a deepened sense of loneliness.

I recently learned there is a term in Third World countries to describe people who come on short-term mission trips. It is not a flattering term, although I think it may be pretty accurate. It's called *poverty tourism*. It describes those of us who come and want to capture our experiences with Third World poverty. We bring our cameras and take pictures of the living conditions and selfies with the children.

I admit that I am personally guilty of poverty tourism. I have taken the pictures of homes made of cardboard and blankets. I took a lot of pictures of Meredith with the children and she took a lot of pictures of me. Taking pictures is not necessarily a problem, but have we ever considered that our cameras may cost more than most of the people we are serving earn in a year? Feeling good about our service should have more to do with the long-term impact we are making than the warm fuzzies we get from selfies with children and the profile pictures we get to put up on our favorite social media sites.

So why do these children run towards every camera they see with a huge smile as they beg to be in the pictures? Some are told they have to by the workers in the orphanage: *The people coming may give the orphanage more money and you need to make them feel welcome.* Some are promised a better chance of adoption. Some are even threatened with punishment. While there are millions of children who need orphanages due to war, famine, and the death of their families, we have to stop feeding the beast and find better solutions.

A friend of mine works with an organization that digs wells to provide clean water to villages where people are literally dying of thirst and need a clean drink of water. On a recent trip he was approached by one of the local woman and asked, "Do orphanages work in the Unites States?"

He was surprised, thought for a minute, and reluctantly responded, "No, not really."

She looked at him and said, "Then why do you think they would work here?" She went on to explain the harsh reality and future of most of the children in Third World orphanages. "When children leave their communities and are placed into an orphanage, they become social outcasts. It does not matter why they are there. It doesn't matter if a parent died of AIDS or was killed in a war. They are no longer members of their village. They are not welcomed back. They do not learn the social system or how to work their family land. When they are too old to stay at the orphanage, most are sent out into the streets. They are given a small amount of money, put on a bus, and sent to another town. They are not accepted back into the village. They don't know anyone and don't have any way of caring for themselves. Most are forced into gangs, the militia, or prostitution."

If you do your research, you will find out this woman is right. There is little hope for a child who ages out of an orphanage in a Third World country. Each day over 38,000 children turn sixteen years of age and are removed from the orphanage because they are too old to stay.[9] That's over 14,000,000 children per year or one child every 2.2 seconds.[9] Here are some of the sobering facts that face these millions of children.

Studies of children in Russia and the Ukraine show that 10-15 percent will commit suicide within two years.[9] Sixty percent of the girls are lured into prostitution. They are often promised jobs in shops and then sold into the sex slave industry.[9] Millions of girls have been trafficked in the sex slave trade simply because they were unfortunate enough to be orphans.[9] Many are sold by the orphanages even before they reach the age of sixteen. Seventy percent of the boys become hardened criminals.[9] They face a life of crime, bouncing in and out of prison. This is the harsh reality that the majority of these children face.

Again, it is not my goal to anger or offend anyone, but some questions have to be asked and some things need to be said. Is a VBS what these children really need? Are the bracelets made with the plan of salvation beads going to offer them a better future? Do they really need to hear they are loved by a complete stranger? Do you think that little girl wonders where that Jesus is you told her about when she's being violated ten to fifteen times a day?

I'm sorry if these questions offend you. Offense is not my goal, but the answers sicken me. We have to deal with the truth. We have to deal with the harsh realities of how our service is horribly missing the mark. Sadly, sometimes the truth is the only thing that will inspire us to do what is right. At least three out of four of these children will end their lives in agonizing pain and suffering as utterly broken people.

Where is the church? Knowing that this is their future, aren't we required to offer better solutions? Are you willing to give up that trip and invest your finances differently now that you know their future? I know these trips create memories that last a lifetime, and we get incredible pictures that remind us to pray for our new friends, but is it worth it? We have to take the truth of their lives into consideration. We have to do what is right.

So what does that look like? What can we really do? How can we help that little girl? Instead of continuing the ongoing exploitation as a result of orphanages, it is our Christian duty to offer more effective strategies. We must serve in ways that rebuild communities and prevent the abuse of these children.

Instead of trying to figure it all out from our own perspective, why don't we start by listening to those we are serving? If we think we have all the answers, are we really recognizing their value or are we perpetuating our superior mind-set? They may know better than we do what they really need.

The woman that was talking with my friend had some incredible ideas about where to start. She gave some extremely insightful suggestions on how we can make a significant difference. "You people with resources, teach us to take care of our own children. Help us keep them in our own communities. If they stay in the community, they won't become social outcasts. They will learn the ways of the village. When they get older, they won't be sent out into the streets. They will be able to reclaim their family land and rebuild their families."

Sounds to me like that woman knows what she's talking about. What she describes reminds me a lot of God's plan for the children of Israel with the Sabbath Year. Like these children, the Israelites had a resource. They had rights to a portion of the land according to their tribe. Leading up to the Sabbath they gained the knowledge of how to operate the fields and vineyards because they worked for someone else. They had built-in relationships when they returned to their tribes. The only thing missing was the opportunity to go home and care for themselves.

This exact same result could be available for children in orphanages if we resourced their neighbors to keep them in their own villages. They already have rights to their family's land. They could gain the knowledge of how the community operates. They could maintain relationships with their neighbors. The only thing missing is their opportunity. Instead of aging out of the orphanage to face a horrible fate, they could be given the chance to rebuild their families.

Doesn't this sound like a better solution? Doesn't this sound like God's plan put into action? Would you be willing to invest your time and energies differently to provide this future for these children? Would you be willing to change the purpose of your trip if this was going to be the result? I believe we all would.

The good news is there are already groups offering these types of services. They are working very hard to keep families together. They are providing food and training if the parent agrees to keep the children. They are providing the free education that is normally not available. They are removing the benefits of dropping children off at the orphanage. They are following God's plan and providing the Four Fundamental Elements.

Business leaders are taking different types of mission trips. They are going to identify local resources that can be used in business. They are setting up stores and selling products made by the locals. Some of these businesses aren't keeping a single penny of the profits for themselves. Instead, they send everything back, so the villagers gain all the benefits.

There is a growing trend and more and more organizations are doing incredible work to alleviate the immediate need while establishing long-term solutions. They are providing the Fundamental Elements and helping people overcome the cause while treating the symptoms. These groups are leading the way and setting the example that many of us need to apply to our own domestic services. They are making systemic changes in the name of Christ.

Groups are investing in local leaders. They are creating microlending opportunities, and each member of the community receives an income by providing a product or service. They are establishing training centers in agriculture and offering families the opportunity to build farming businesses. They are setting up sustainable solutions. Hopeless villages are being rebuilt.

Other ministries are finding locals who have natural gifts and are putting them into places of leadership. They are investing in their education. They are resourcing them to build hospitals, schools, and homes. Volunteers are still taking trips, but they don't go in and take over. They work side by side with the locals, under local leadership.

This is a better representation of God's plan. We must provide services that offer hope. We must show them a Jesus who offers them dignity today as well as life everlasting. This is the answer. It may not be as fun for us, but it works and God gets the glory.

DISCUSSION QUESTIONS

1. What experience have you had serving the poorest of the poor in Third World countries?
2. How does consumerism play into our desire to go and serve others in Third World countries?
3. What are better ways to spend the billions of dollars to more effectively treat the causes of poverty?
4. Why do you believe we have never been told the truth about the future of over 75 percent of children living in orphanages?
5. How has your opinion of Third World orphanages changed with the understanding that roughly 80 percent of orphans have at least one parent living?
6. What are some actions we can take to ensure that orphans receive better care?

CHAPTER 12

FINAL THOUGHTS

B reaking the Broken presents an overview of God's plan for us to serve broken people in ways that represent His heart. This is His plan for justice to restore the hurting and poor. These are His guidelines to renew their lives and help them find dignity and value. God's plan offers hope.

We have seen the what, who, why, and where. We have even covered the how. The only thing left to understand is the *when*. Before we get to that, let's have a quick review. Let's make sure we have put all of these pieces into place.

God had a plan for people to independently provide for their own needs. God's plan included Four Fundamental Elements. Three of these Elements allow us to live and one allows us to have a full life. The first three Elements are: Resources, Opportunity, and Instruction. The last, and by far the most important, is Relationships. God used these Four Fundamental Elements throughout Scripture to guide His people, and Jesus used them in His own earthly life and ministry.

We have learned there are three different groups of people that we identify as "poor": the Can'ts, the Don'ts, and the Won'ts. We now understand that their poverty is based upon their abilities to gain and use God's plan to care for themselves. We have seen that our response to the poor is based upon their individual situations. We care for the Can'ts, those who *cannot* gain the first three Fundamental Elements, and we provide for them in ways that allow them to have the dignity to do everything they are able to do for themselves. We provide access to resources, opportunity, and instruction for the Don'ts, those who *do not* have at least one of the first three Fundamental Elements, to gain the missing elements and provide for their own needs. We stop systematically supporting the Won'ts, those who have the first three Fundamental Elements and *will not* use them, and we display tough love by encouraging and even requiring them to care for themselves. We serve each and every one of these people through the fourth Fundamental Element: Relationships.

God established work as the means by which people would provide for their own needs and the needs of their family. He required Adam to work in the Garden of Eden even before the fall. He continued to require people to work throughout the Old and New Testaments. Through work we gain confidence, value, and purpose. Work allows us to see ourselves as His creations, uniquely designed with dignity and worth.

We reviewed ways to follow God's plan in both domestic and international ministries. We have seen that we must meet the physical needs for the Can'ts, but this should only be done as a bridge for the Don'ts. We learned that our felt-need services should be available for the purpose of establishing long-term solutions. We have seen the pros and cons of our service and some unintended consequences of ministering in ways that may feel good, but don't represent God. We have seen ways that our services are actually making things worse, causing pain, and breaking the broken.

The last thing we need to cover is the question of *when*. Let me give you the short answer—*now*. We are called to follow God's plan all day, every day. It is not something that is reserved for special occasions. It can't be used for one-time events that our churches hold in the community. God's plan is part of our everyday lives.

Paul tells us, in Romans 12:1-2, that our "spiritual act of worship" is not what we do for a few minutes before a sermon on Sunday morning. Our worship is the way we live our lives every single day as we represent Christ to a lost and broken world. We worship God by living a holy response to His love and calling. He calls us to turn away from what the world says is right and live in ways that He says are holy. God's plan is part of that holy calling.

There are just a few more things we need to cover before we bring this to a close. A couple of things we need to deal with in advance. Some things that can help or hinder the application of God's plan. Let's look at those so we can represent His plan in healthy ways, then we'll look at the results of God's plan. We'll see why His plan is so important in our ministries.

The first thing I want to cover is the mutual responsibility we have with those we serve. This is not a one-sided relationship. This is not just a give and take. We are called to clothe the naked, feed the hungry, and visit those who are suffering, but they have a responsibility as well. They are called to do something with the resources we invest in their lives.

Every lesson we have learned about caring for ourselves; working six days, being responsible, not eating our brother's bread without paying for it, are not only intended for those who have money. Those are part of God's plan for all of humanity. Those we serve must take ownership of their own lives. These commands in Scripture are not written strictly for a certain segment of society. They are universal. They are for everyone, including those we serve.

The second part we need to understand is that change is not easy. It is a long, painstaking process. It may take years and years for people to gain the Fundamental Elements and properly apply them to their lives. There will be ups and downs. There is no pill that can be prescribed to suddenly equip individuals with all of the Fundamental Elements at once. It takes time.

We need to understand this is not an overnight process. Therefore, we must develop a growth model. Someone raised in a lifestyle of poverty, who has learned from childhood that society will provide for them, may not be too happy when they hear the word *no*. They may get angry. They may start rumors. They may walk away.

It's OK. Early in ministry we learned the difference between a prodigal son and a lost sheep. We learned to look at the evidence of their lives and decide whether they innocently wandered away or made the conscious choice to return to their old way of life. Sometimes we need to go find them and bring them back. Other times we need to watch, pray, and wait patiently for their return, but we don't quit.

God puts an extremely high value on how we care for the poor. Our response to their need is so important, He tied blessings and curses to our service. If we follow His commands, it will be counted as righteousness. If we don't follow His commands, we will be cursed. God has a history of punishing those who don't properly care for the poor.

I don't know what you learned, but I learned Sodom and Gomorrah were destroyed because of their sexual sin. It is common knowledge they were sexually perverse. The account of their sin is plainly written in Genesis, but was that their only offense? There is no doubt they were detestable, but was sexual sin the only charge the Lord made against Sodom and Gomorrah? Let's review what Scripture records.

> Then the LORD said, "The outcry against Sodom and Gomorrah is immense, and their sin is extremely serious. I will go down to see if what they have done

justifies the cry that has come up to Me. If not, I will
find out." (Gen. 18:20-21)

The remainder of Genesis 18 provides details of the conversation between the Lord and Abraham as Abraham negotiates to save the people of Sodom and Gomorrah. Abraham gets the Lord to agree that if as few as ten righteous people can be found, He will not destroy the cities. The Lord's angels go to investigate, but the men of Sodom want to rape them. Lot tries to stop the men and even offers his virgin daughters as replacements, but they won't back down and threaten to do even worse things to Lot. This is where we pick it back up.

> *Then the angels said to Lot, "Do you have anyone else*
> *here: a son-in-law, your sons and daughters, or*
> *anyone else in the city who belongs to you? Get them*
> *out of this place, for we are about to destroy this*
> *place because the outcry against its people is so*
> *great before the LORD, that the LORD has sent us to*
> *destroy it."* (Gen. 19:12-13)

As I read through this passage I saw something that caught my attention. What was the "outcry" the Lord heard against Sodom and Gomorrah? Was it their detestable sin? Who was crying out? As I thought through these questions I remembered a passage in Deuteronomy.

> *"When you make a loan of any kind to your neighbor,*
> *do not enter his house to collect what he offers as*
> *security. You must stand outside while the man you*
> *are making the loan to brings the security out to you.*
> *If he is a poor man, you must not sleep in the garment*
> *he has given as security. Be sure to return it to him at*
> *sunset. Then he will sleep in it and bless you, and this*
> *will be counted as righteousness to you before the*
> *LORD your God." Do not oppress a hired hand who is*

poor and needy, whether one of your brothers or one of the foreigners residing within a town in your land. You are to pay him his wages each day before the sun sets, because he is poor and depends on them. Otherwise he will cry out to the LORD against you, and you will be held guilty. (Deut. 24:10-15)

When we treat the poor unjustly or we add to their pain, they will cry out to the Lord and He will find us guilty. This same warning is found in other places in Scripture. If we care for the poor correctly, He will bless us and it is counted as righteousness. If we mistreat them, they will cry out and we will be held responsible. The poor cried out against the people of Sodom and Gomorrah and the Lord heard their cry and investigated to see if it was justified. Why would I make that connection?

During my sabbatical I was doing some research on this subject and followed a reference to a passage in Ezekiel 16. This chapter records a list of sins the people of Jerusalem had committed. They began partnering with people who worshipped other gods. They were behaving as prostitutes with other countries. They were taking the wealth God had given them and using it to make false idols. They were sacrificing their children to these false gods. Then Ezekiel says their sin was worse than the sin of Sodom.

> *"As I live, declares the Lord GOD, your sister Sodom and her daughters have not done as you and your daughters have done. Behold, this was the guilt of your sister Sodom: she and her daughters had pride, excess of food, and prosperous ease, but did not aid the poor and needy."* (Ezek. 16:48-49 ESV)

Yes, Sodom was a sexually perverse town, but Ezekiel points out another sin. They had everything they wanted: food, comfort, and security, but it is not a sin to have food, comfort, and security.

Their sin was that they were filled with pride and "did not aid the poor and the needy." Verse 50 goes on to say that they believed they were superior to others and committed "detestable things." They occupied their time with gluttonous behavior: self-satisfaction, opulence, greed, and living to fulfill every one of their sinful desires—all at the expense of providing aid to the poor.

The key to this passage is the word *aid*. What does it mean to "aid the poor and needy"? Does it mean to feed the hungry, give a drink to the thirsty, or provide a bed for the homeless? Does it mean to clothe the naked, care for the sick, or visit those in prison? The Hebrew word translated as "aid" (in other translations "support or strengthen") means "to prevail." It means you are making something strong or restoring it to strength. The people neglected God's plan to care for the poor by restoring them to strength. The sin the people of Sodom committed is very similar to what we read in Amos 2. In this section God is telling the different tribes, and the entire nation of Israel, the offenses they are guilty of committing.

> *The LORD says: "I will not relent from punishing Israel for three crimes, even four, because they sell a righteous person for silver and a needy person for a pair of sandals. They trample the heads of the poor on the dust of the ground and block the path of the needy. A man and his father have sexual relations with the same girl, profaning My holy name. They stretch out beside every altar on garments taken as collateral, and in the house of their God, they drink wine obtained through fines." (Amos 2:6-8)*

Israel was deep in sin and in this list of crimes, there were accusations against them concerning how they treated the poor. They sold the needy, they trampled their head in the dust, they blocked their path, and they kept their garments overnight. The first and second sins are no brainers, we don't sell people or trample their heads in the dust. The fourth sin was covered in chapter 5 when we studied the passage in Deuteronomy 24:12 concerning returning a coat that had been taken as collateral so the poor man could sleep in it. The third sin listed is the one that requires further study in view of God's plan. What does it mean to "block the path of the needy"? To answer this question, let's continue to see what God has to say about caring for the poor. How are we supposed to serve Him? What are God's priorities? What are His instructions? Do you think He wants traditions and sacrifices…or actions that reflect His heart?

> *"Is not this the kind of fasting I have chosen: to loose the chains of injustice and untie the cords of the yoke, to set the oppressed free and break every yoke? Is it not to share your food with the hungry and to provide the poor wanderer with shelter—when you see the naked, to clothe them, and not to turn away from your own flesh and blood? Then your light will break forth like the dawn, and your healing will quickly appear; then your righteousness will go before you, and the glory of the Lord will be your rear guard. Then you will call, and the Lord will answer; you will cry for help, and He will say: Here am I. If you do away with the yoke of oppression, with the pointing finger and malicious talk, and if you spend yourselves in behalf of the hungry and satisfy the needs of the oppressed, then your light will rise in the darkness, and your night will become like the noonday. The Lord will guide you always; He will satisfy your needs in a sun-scorched land and will strengthen your frame. You will be like a well-watered garden, like a spring whose waters never fail."* (Isa. 58:6-11 NIV)

God's desire is laid out in these verses. God calls us to "loose the chains of injustice." Chains are used to hold people down. He instructs us to "untie the cords of the yoke." I love this imagery. A yoke is a wooden crosspiece that is fastened over the necks of animals and attached to the plow or cart they are to pull. We are called to remove the things that are holding them in bondage. We are supposed to set them free so they can care for themselves.

Yes, we are to feed the hungry, give drink to the thirsty, and provide a bed for the homeless. We are called to clothe the naked, care for the sick, and visit those in prison, but God doesn't tell us to stop there. God calls us to treat the symptom as we address the cause and set people free to care for themselves. We are to "meet the need" of the oppressed. We meet their need the same way Jesus did. He removed the reason they were unable to care for themselves. Social justice does not do these things. God's plan is the answer.

So what is the end game? Why is all of this so important? Why did God create such a clear structure around services to the poor? Why did God attach blessings and curses to these services? Because God had a result that He was going to accomplish.

What is the result of putting everything we have learned into practice? Scripture gives us two very distinct benefits of serving God's way. The first is found in Isaiah 61. I believe it is God giving us a little glimpse as to what will happen when we remove chains, untie yokes, and meet the needs of the oppressed like we are told to do in Isaiah 58. God tells us what we can expect if we provide others with the Four Fundamental Elements and serve the poor according to His plan.

> *The Spirit of the Lord GOD is on Me, because the LORD has anointed Me to bring good news to the poor. He has sent Me to heal the brokenhearted, to proclaim liberty to the captives and freedom to the prisoners; to proclaim the year of the LORD's*

189

favor, and the day of our God's vengeance; to comfort all who mourn, to provide for those who mourn in Zion; to give them a crown of beauty instead of ashes, festive oil instead of mourning, and splendid clothes instead of despair. And they will be called righteous trees, planted by the LORD to glorify Him. (Isa. 61:1-3)

What is this good news He calls us to bring to the poor? That they will be released from the things that hold them down. The brokenhearted will be healed. Those who are held captive will no longer be oppressed. Prisoners will find freedom. We are called to heal the broken with the good news that God loves them and they are valued. We must help them see themselves as worth something more than what this world can offer. The result of this type of ministry is found in the very next verse.

They shall build up the ancient ruins; they shall raise up the former devastations; they shall repair the ruined cities, the devastations of many generations. (v. 4)

This is the way God rebuilds people. If we heal the broken and set them free to care for themselves, *they* will rebuild their own communities. *They* will build up the ancient ruins. *They* will raise up the former devastations. *They* shall repair the ruined cities, the devastations of many generations.

Our call is to pour our resources into building up the broken so they can learn that they have a purpose and find their value from God. When we provide services that restore them, *they* will begin to rebuild themselves. *They* will raise up leaders. *They* will overcome the negative effects of generational poverty.

We represent the Great Physician. He is Jehovah Rapha, the God who heals. Presenting Jehovah Rapha, as we serve the broken, is what we are called to do. We are His hands and feet. He is the author of the answers.

Doctors take a Hippocratic Oath to create standards regarding their service. As representatives of the Great Physician, maybe we should do the same. Here's what I suggest.

A Hippocratic Oath for Ministry

In the name of our Lord Jesus Christ,
I will view others with dignity and purpose,
as men and women created in the image of God.
I pledge that I will not steal their self-respect and
will only provide what they truly need.
I promise to never give them what they can gain on their own,
and above all, in all ministry endeavors,
I will do no harm.

While providing self-sufficiency to the poor is a good work, is that all God is calling us to do? Does He want nothing more than for us to teach GED classes in prisons? Maybe God's greatest desire is for us to help people gain life skills and learn to care for themselves. If that is the case, then the church might as well get out of the way and let others do the work. That brings us to the real results of following God's plan to equip people with the Four Fundamental Elements and free them to care for themselves.

> As they were leaving Jericho, a large crowd followed
> Him. There were two blind men sitting by the road.
> When they heard that Jesus was passing by, they
> cried out, "Lord, have mercy on us, Son of David!" The
> crowd told them to keep quiet, but they cried out all
> the more, "Lord, have mercy on us, Son of David!"
> Jesus stopped, called them, and said, "What do you
> want Me to do for you?" "Lord," they said to Him,
> "open our eyes!" Moved with compassion, Jesus

*touched their eyes. Immediately they could see, and
they followed Him.* (Matt. 20:29-33)

This is an incredible passage. These blind men knew Jesus
was walking by and they begged for mercy. Mercy means we treat
people kindly instead of harshly. These men were asking for Jesus
to treat them better than they deserved. Everyone in Jerusalem
provided financial support for these men, but they were asking
Jesus for more than the societal norm.

I love Jesus' style. He didn't jump in and give instructions
telling people what to do. He didn't tell those following Him to
give these men money. Instead, He asked a question that got to
the root of their request: "What do you *want* me to do for you?"
He was revealing their hearts. They were Can'ts, but His question
exposed their motivation. When healed, would they be Won'ts?

At that point, they could have asked for anything. They knew
who Jesus was and knew the power He had to change their lives.
They could have asked for new sandals to wear as they walked to
the temple to beg. They could have asked for housing or food or a
guide dog. They could have even asked for enough money to pay
for everything they would ever need, but they didn't ask for any
of these things. Rather, they asked for their sight.

I have often wondered how Jesus would have responded if
these men had asked for anything other than their sight.
I wonder if He would have been "moved with compassion" or if
He would have rebuked them. Would He have healed them, or
used the opportunity as a teaching moment for His disciples?
They asked Jesus to remove the obstacle that was standing in
their way of being productive members of society who could care
for their own needs. They asked for their sight and moved with
compassion, Jesus healed them.

What do you think was the result of this interaction that
Jesus had with these men? They received their sight and they
followed Him! That is the result of us properly presenting God's

plan. People are looking for real answers from a Jesus who truly cares about them today and for eternity. When we meet the real needs of hurting and broken people, they want more. People who are healed in the name of Jesus want to follow Jesus.

Living out God's plan is not easy, but it's worth it. It is great to see men and women get jobs. I go to bed every night with a smile on my face when people gain their independence. I loved watching a young lady become the first women in her family to ever walk across that stage, receive her diploma, and graduate from high school. Helping someone move out of the projects and into their own home is satisfying, but nothing can compare to leading someone to Jesus.

There is a rising movement in society to help people learn life skills and find jobs. The goal of the movement is to rebuild poor neighborhoods and teach people to care for themselves. Many churches have joined this effort. While this is noble work, many of these community development efforts miss the mark. As believers, helping someone become self-sufficient is not our ultimate goal. If we feed the poor, clothe the naked, and visit those in prison, but don't introduce them to Jesus, what was the point? If we help people get off government assistance, gain an education, find a job, build a business, buy a house, and change the legacy of their family, but they do not meet Jesus, then we have failed! A successful life is meaningless if it results in an eternity in hell.

The end of the book of Matthew records Jesus talking to His disciples. His instruction recorded there is commonly referred to as the Great Commission. These are His marching orders to His followers. This is their charge as His representatives. This is His command.

> *"Go, therefore, and make disciples of all nations,*
> *baptizing them in the name of the Father and of the*
> *Son and of the Holy Spirit, teaching them to observe*

everything I have commanded you. And remember, I
am with you always, to the end of the age."
(Matt. 28: 19-20)

Yes, God cares about the poor. He wants them to be restored. He wants them to break free from the chains that are holding them down, but He wants more. We are required to give them more. We are told to point people to Jesus. God's plan points people to Him.

He wants a relationship with them. Jesus didn't go to Calvary for poor communities to be rebuilt. God sent His son to restore broken relationships. Serving the poor according to God's plan helps build those relationships. The fourth Fundamental Element is what God wants with people.

Now let's go. Let's go into our communities and show people they have value because of Jesus. Let's go to the uttermost parts of the world and show them a loving God by equipping them to care for themselves. Let's go with God's truth. Let's go with God's plan. Let's go and heal the broken...

AND THEY WILL FOLLOW HIM!

DISCUSSION QUESTIONS

1. What can you do to make your life a "spiritual act of worship"?
2. What crimes would God find against you based upon your service to the poor?
3. Based on your reading of Isaiah, what are some ways you can live out the call to serve the poor?
4. Which part of the Hippocratic Oath will be the hardest for you to fulfill?
5. How has your previous service helped introduce those you served to Jesus?
6. How can our services better present a Jesus who loves the poor and cares about their dignity, value, and worth?
7. What will you do with Jesus' call to *go*?

INDEX

Chapter 2 – God Had a Plan
1. http://www.livescience.com/18800-loneliness-health-problems.html
2. http://thebrain.mcgill.ca/flash/capsules/histoire_bleu06.html

Chapter 3 – God's Plan in the Old Testament
1. Quote from Nietzsche's is a derivation from Beyond Good and Evil. Aphorism number 183
   "Not that you lied to me but that I no longer believe you has shaken me."

Chapter 5 – God's Plan and The Poor
1. http://www.un.org/waterforlifedecade/food_security.shtml
2. http://www.unicef.org/mdg/childmortality.html
3. http://www.unicef.org/sowc06/press/who.php
4. https://www.census.gov/prod/2012pubs/acsbr11-01.pdf
5. https://www.census.gov/prod/2012pubs/acsbr11-08.pdf
6. http://quickfacts.census.gov/qfd/states/47/4752006.html

Chapter 7 – Why Work?
1. https://sleepfoundation.org/sites/default/files/2005_summary_of_findings.pdf
2. www.people.uncw.edu/robertsonj/SEC210/Maslow.pdf
3. http://academic.udayton.edu/jackbauer/Readings%20595/Koltko-Rivera%2006%20trans%20self-act%20copy.pdf
4. www.presidency.ucsb.edu/ws/?pid=24504

Chapter 8 – Application
1. www.thecookery.org/about-2/brett-swayn
2. John Perkins, With Justice for All: A Strategy for Community Development (Grand Rapids, MI, Baker Books 2011)

Chapter 9 – Guiding Principles
1. www.theodorerooseveltcenter.org/learn-About-TR/TR-Quotes.aspx

Chapter 11 – International Ministries
1. http://www.acf.hhs.gov/sites/default/files/cb/afcarsreport22.pdf
2. Princeton University sociologist Robert Wuthnow (per footnote comment contained in "GodSpace07" in Mission Maker Magazine 2007, Minneapolis MN: STEM Press)
3. http://www.worldbank.org/en/topic/poverty/overview
4. http://www.replace-campaign.org/harm.html
5. http://www.theguardian.com/society/2009/nov/24/save-the-children-orphans-report
6. http://www.unicef.org/aids/files/aids_TakingEvidencetoImpact.pdf
7. https://www.savethechildren.org.uk/sites/default/files/docs/Keeping_Children_Out_of_Harmful_Institutions_Final_20.11.09_1.pdf
8. http://www.replace-campaign.org/harm.html
9. www.hfgf.org/statistics.pdf

ABOUT THE AUTHOR

Rob Kendall is a husband, father, grandfather, speaker, and ministry consultant. When he co-founded Against the Grain with his wife Meredith, he brought years of experience in business leadership to the ministry. The Kendall's co-authored The 180 Program. The 180 Program is a biblically-based, life recovery series of studies that are spreading across the country. These studies are used in churches, jails, prisons, transitional homes, homeless shelters, and crisis pregnancy and recovery centers to provide hope through Christ to thousands of people every year.

Today, Rob remains involved with Against the Grain as the Founding Director and Chairman of the Board. Rob is the Founder and President of Renewing the Mind Network, a national ministry that equips the church to be the church by providing Biblical solutions to real life struggles.

To inquire about speaking engagements or share thoughts on the book, please e-mail Rob@BreakingTheBroken.com

To read Rob's blogs and get involved in the discussion visit www.breakingthebroken.com

THE 180 PROGRAM

The New Beginnings Study
This foundational study leads students to identify, understand, and overcome the thoughts, feelings, behaviors, and patterns that are the root cause of their struggles and find victory through a personal relationship with Christ.

Job Readiness
There is more to getting a job and building a career than writing a good resume. This study teaches the students that if their life is not "together" their job won't be either.

Budgeting 101
A simply explained budgeting system specifically designed to get struggling families on the right track.

Relationships and Parenting
"My behavior doesn't hurt anybody but me." That excuse is challenged as we learn that our choices and behaviors affect others, including our children.

Leadership
The experiences and examples from childhood effect our abilities to lead. This study helps us overcome those bad patterns and become the leaders we were created to be.

For more information on The 180 Program or to make a donation, please visit www.the180program.org